IMMIGRATION
and the
American Dream

Suhayl Jamil Farha, M.D.

"Dr. Jim"

DEDICATION

To my parents, Jamil Farhat Farha and Wadia Mikhael Farha,
who were willing to invest all of the family's property in sending
their two sons to the United States,
to realize the American Dream for themselves,
and for their siblings,
and for the generations that would follow.

And to my sister, Violette, who pioneered our way to America
and made it possible for us to attain the American Dream.

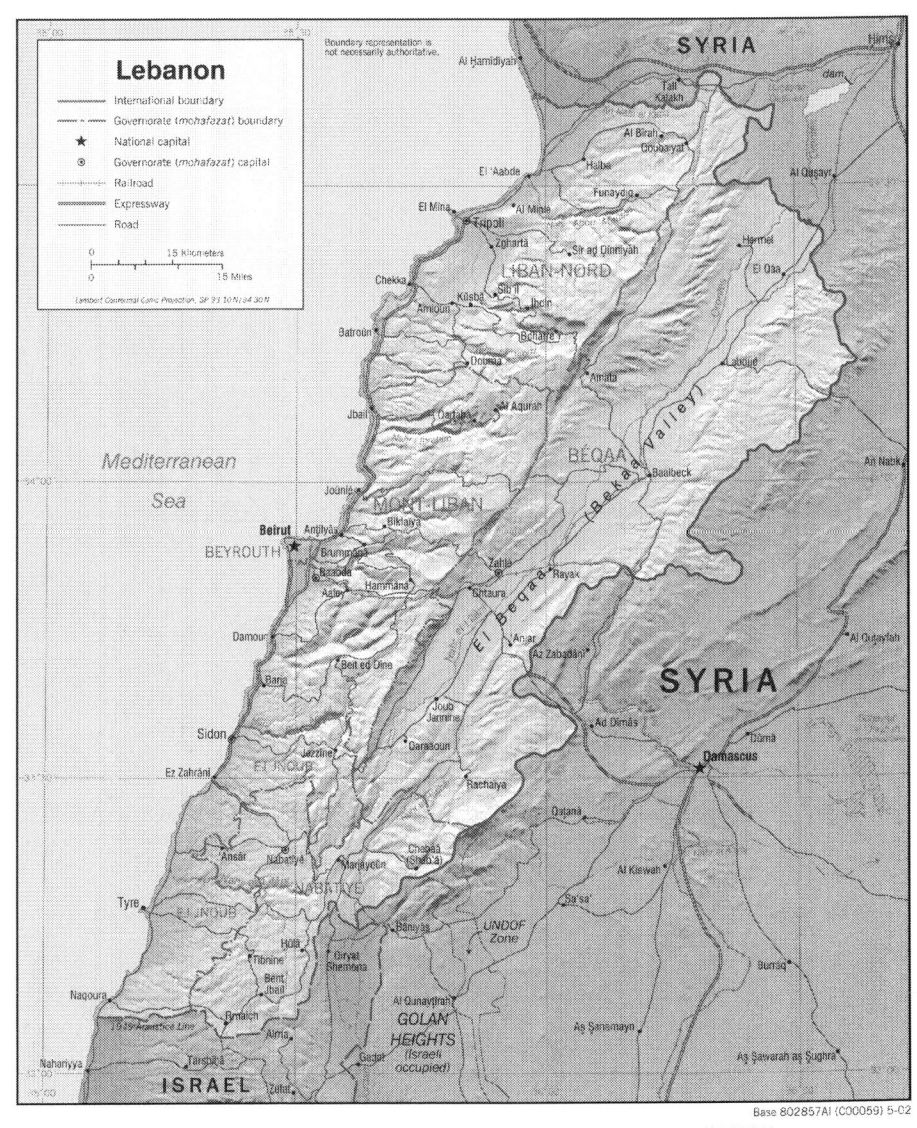

Lebanon

———— International boundary
— ~ ~ Governorate (mohafazat) boundary
★ National capital
◉ Governorate (mohafazat) capital
·········· Railroad
▓▓▓▓▓ Expressway
———— Road

0   15 Kilometers
0   15 Miles

Lambert Conformal Conic Projection, SP 33 10 N / 34 30 N

SYRIA

Al Hamidiyah
Tall Kalakh
dam
Al Birah
Qoubayat
Al 'Aabde
Haiba
Al Qasayr
El Mina
Tripoli
Al Mina
Funaydiq
Zgharta
Sir ad Dinniyah
Hermel
Chekka
Kūsba
Sir il
Ihdin
El Qaa
Amioun
LIBAN-NORD
Batroün
Bcharré
Douma
Latqiyé
Jbail
Dartāla
Al Aqurah
Amiata
Ain Nabk
Aïnta
BÉQAA
Mediterranean
Jounié
Joúnié
Baalbeck
Sea
MONT-LIBAN
Biklaiya
Beirut
Antilyâs
BEYROUTH
Brummāna
Baabda
Zahla
Hammāna
Shtaura
Rayak
Aqley
Damour
Anjar
Al Qutayfah
Baria
Beit ed Dine
Az Zabadāni
Joub
SYRIA
Sidon
Jarmine
Ad Dimās
Dūma
Jezzine
Caraaoun
Damascus
Ez Zahrâni
EL JNOUB
Rachaiya
Qatana
Chebaa
Al Kiswah
(Shab'a)
'Ansar
NABATYE
Nabatiye
Marjayoûn
Bâ'sa
Tyre
Marjayoún
Bāniyās
UNDOF
Zone
Burāq
Hula
Tibnine
Giryat
Shemona
Bent
Jbail
Naqoura
Al Qunaytirah
Ismailh
Aş Şanamayn
Alma
GOLAN
HEIGHTS
Nahariyya
Tarshiha
(Israeli
Aş Şawarah aş Sughra
occupied)
Gadar
1949 Armistice Line
ISRAEL
Zafat

CONTENTS

Note from the Author

I have been very fortunate to be a part of this country. I think that the American people are the kindest people in the world. I have had contact with the French and the British, and generally I didn't care much for them. Often they were very arrogant. Of course, not everyone in every other country is worthy of disdain and not everyone in this country is worthy of my respect. But I have met so many kind people in America, so many people who helped me out when I needed it without even a second thought, that I feel pretty well justified in saying that America is the greatest country in the world.

I was very "foreign" early in the game. Once I became more Americanized, while I was going through medical school, I became more aware of how different I was when I started out. But I hardly noticed in the beginning stages. The American people were so good to me and didn't treat me any different from a natural-born citizen. Even those who were not well educated were kind, offering me rides and other help. It fostered in me a great love for my country, and to this day I resent anyone badmouthing America. We have it good here with the American competitiveness and the American individualism. Those things have helped to make the average American exceptional. He's a very productive, independent citizen who is well educated and capable to reaching heights the world has never seen before. America has done that for me. I feel very fortunate to have had the opportunity to come to America to get an education.

Of course, this was all made possible thanks to the support of my family. My brother George and I were blessed to have two loving parents who were willing to give up everything to send their two youngest sons to a foreign country to gain their educations. Without the support of our family, George and I would never have been able to succeed.

Thanks to people like my parents, immigrants, especially those who have come here to better themselves, have contributed a great deal to this country. They educated themselves and propelled themselves into positions of leadership in the country. In turn, they have impacted American communities in a big way, just like high tide lifts all boats.

The most fortunate thing that's happened to me is coming to America. It made its mark on me. I hope I have contributed a little to my community in return.

Chapter 1: Early Childhood

Jdeidat Marjeyoun, a small town in Southern Lebanon, is a picturesque place. Meaning literally "Plain of Water," or more poetically "Meadow of Springs," its fields are green and rich with vegetation, rolling gently at the foot of Mount Hermon. To the west are the remains of Beaufort Castle, reminiscent of a time come and gone, and the summits of the Mount Lebanon range, which stretch out to the north, encasing the plains that trail toward Golan Heights. The landscape is a painter's dream.

At 500 meters above sea level, the weather there resembles California. The winters are cool and short, the summers nice and dry. But during fall and spring, it stays a balmy 70 degrees, perfect to explore the wide expanses of marshlands and plains. During some months, you can experience two seasons in one day if you simply climbed high enough in the mountains to experience the frigid temperatures.

Although in Lebanon, Marjeyoun used to be a predominately Christian town. Religious fights between Muslims and Christians were very few and far between. It was an enclave, and its people had the protection of their neighbors of similar beliefs.

In my childhood, Marjeyoun had many beautiful things. But it was missing a few of the niceties I enjoyed in America as an adult.

Like running water. And electricity. And, by extension, things like hot showers, air conditioning, refrigeration, and access to proper medicine. Basically anything that present-day Americans see as necessary for survival was not available. At least not while I was growing up there. The only fancy thing we had was indoor plumbing.

This was my home for most of my childhood. It is where I was born, where I took my first steps, where I made my first friends, and largely where I developed as a person. I was living in a tiny stone house with my seven other siblings—Nazik, Nazmiah, Fayez, Suad, Georgette, Violette, and George—and my parents. There were two bedrooms and a salon. All eight of the children slept on the floor of one bedroom while the other was reserved for my parents. Luckily, two of my sisters were married by the time I turned two years old and moved out, so we had a bit more room after that. It was in that little, cramped house that I learned to respect my elders, to stay out of trouble, and to find an appreciation for education.

I didn't learn those things all at once, though. I was a particularly active (and some might say mildly troublesome) child. I loved to explore the country, play in the dirt, and experience new things. As the youngest of the bunch, my older siblings looked out for me, giving me pointers and trying to keep me on the right path. I often didn't listen to them. I'm sure that Georgette (who was born fifth) lost more than a little hair because of me. She took the most responsibility in looking after me. She was a very strict girl and she was always upset if I came to the house filthy. She would scrub me until my skin turned red. But I suppose I might have deserved it. My family says I'm the reason she went bald later in life!

There weren't a lot of ways to get into trouble in such a little village. Maybe you would act up at school. Maybe you would trespass on a neighbor's apple tree. They were harmless, if somewhat mischievous, acts of little children. You'd be punished by your father, which could be quite the harrowing experience, but there was no lasting damage done in either the act or the punishment.

Even despite the limited ways to get in trouble, I managed to get into a lot of it, more than the other children in my family did. George, my older brother who was born seventh, was the closest to my age, and because of that we had a lot of things in common. The youngest in the family were always taken care of by the older siblings, and so he and I got a great deal of attention and advice from the other six children. But in personality, he and I were often very different. Although he was only about four years my elder, he acted more like my father than like my brother. I've always acted and felt a good deal younger than George.

George was a conforming entity. He didn't like to play in the dirt. He didn't even like to work in the dirt—he never helped mother in the garden like I did. I loved to play outside and work outside and get dirty. It was fun. But George had other interests—for instance, he sang very well. And since he was older than me, he didn't like it when I tried to tag along with him and his friends. And so, although George and I became best friends later in life, our differences at a young age were accentuated.

We weren't the only ones who noticed our differences, for sure. In my culture, we very often compliment, or perhaps even over-compliment, people's strengths or defining characteristics. For George, it was the fact that he was tall and good looking. People made that known to him, and so he felt it was an image to be proud of and one that he had to keep up. And so he acted accordingly. For me, it was the fact that I was powerful and strong. People made that known to me, and so I felt it was an image to be proud of and one that I had to keep up. And so I acted accordingly. I became rather rambunctious.

As a grown up, I realize the fallacy of the emphasis my family placed on me. They emphasized my physical strength rather than my mental aptitude, and so that's what I focused on as well. I felt that I had to demonstrate my strength everywhere I went. Naturally, I managed to get into a lot of mischief that way, but—just like the other kids in town—I didn't get into any big trouble like taking drugs or killing anyone. But I did have plenty of "fights." I never backed down from a fight, and I can't say that I never picked one myself.

Aside from that, I think the worst thing I ever did was drink alcohol once or twice as a teenager. These vices were well within the bounds of servility.

When I wasn't getting into trouble, though, I did normal little boy things. Most of the people in the area knew each other well, so it wasn't hard for me to make friends. I was especially close to the boys in the Tiar family. We found ways to keep each other entertained. I didn't have many toys, but my friends and I kept ourselves entertained with marbles, a yo-yo, and kites. If we got bored of that, we'd grab empty cans from the trash and cook in them, pretending we were soldiers. I also did a lot of exploring.

Running water came to Marjeyoun around 1948. It was only running a minute amount, but it was a big improvement. In fact, it left enough of an impression on me that I still remember the name of the man who came by to install it. (But, come to think of it, the fact that he had only one eye might have had an equal impression on my young mind.) Anyway, he put some water in a reservoir on top of the house. Never mind the fact that moss grew in it. After the system was installed, we could do things like take a shower for the first time in our lives. Of course, the water was cold (until we got a charcoal-powered heating tank to mix hot water with the cold water in the tank) but it was a big deal to me and my family then.

Lebanon was poor when I was growing up. I was born just after the Great Depression hit. America wasn't the only country that had an economic collapse—not by a long shot. Everything in my country was rationed, and a lot of goods weren't even available at all. If there were such a thing as a fourth-world country, Lebanon would have been it. But my father was making a little money from the land we owned and the crops we planted. We always had enough to eat, enough grains anyway. But even though my family was considered middle class, my father was very careful with our money.

I can still remember a particularly small incident that left a large impression on me. It happened when I was very young. There was a new trend amongst all of my other middle class buddies to buy a certain kind of sandals. One by one each of my friends went and bought a pair and soon I was convinced that they were cool, too, and I really wanted a pair of my own. They were rather inexpensive—they cost less than a dollar in American money. But when I went to ask my father if I could buy a pair of sandals, he told me no. He didn't want to spend the money on something so frivolous. I didn't talk back (by that time I'd learned not to), and I really did understand his reasoning. But it's something that's changed the way I look at my childhood and the way I look at financial matters.

I'm not entirely sure what it was that my father did for work. I think he recorded deeds for the area our little town was in, but I can't be sure. He had a lot of connections to government and high-up officials, but he didn't actually work for the government. He tried to, once, though. He ran for Congress, but he dropped out of the race after only a short while. It quickly became evident to him that the entire system was rigged.

You see, there was a Shi'ite family in the area who could trace their ancestry all the way back directly to the Prophet Muhammad. And this family had a list. This list cost a lot of money to get on, somewhere in the ballpark of two to three hundred thousand dollars. But if you were on the list, you got elected. It was simple as that.

It wasn't only that way for Congress; that's how elections worked. There were only three or four guys who qualified for anything, the big names from big families. If you weren't born into one of those families, you had no chance. And everything is based on religion, even the constitution. The President from Lebanon has to be a Christian Maronite. The Prime Minister of Defense had to be a Druze. And because there's no mobility in the system, there's no industry. The only ones who pay taxes are the ones who work for the government. And worst of all, they didn't even try to hide bribery, they just call it "good will."

Needless to say, my father wasn't making very much of an income with his job, especially when you factor in having to pay for a family of eight children. Most of the money and resources my family pulled in and used came from the family land. It was inherited land that had been in the family for a long time. It was shared with a few cousins and a few other families, but it was a lot of land, and it was fertile. We sowed a lot of crops—mostly barley, and wheat—which we used for our own food and which we sold from the basement of our house to other families in town.

Farming in Golan Heights was a bit more involved than it is in America. There were a lot of smugglers in the area, and my father had to protect the crops from them as best he could. It was laborious work, even though he had help. He might have hired a few hands, but mostly the help came from family and family friends in the area. My father was a well-liked and respected man, and people were willing to give him their time. And so the lot of them spent two or three months out of the year simply protecting the crops. Half of the crops usually ended up being taken despite their efforts. But Father put in the time and the work to provide for us.

My mother and the girls put in a lot of time and effort to keep the family going as well by helping around the house. To this day it amazes me that they were able to do what they did. There were no grocery stores and no supermarkets. We had to make our own soap and our own bread, and since raising animals was costly and time-consuming (and space-consuming), we seldom had fresh meat. We owned a few chickens, which gave us eggs. There were vegetable stands, but they were up only during the summer. For most of the year, you depended on yourself and a few little shops, usually run out of homes, which had maybe a sack of potatoes, or corn, or other grain that you can come and buy a little bit here and there. My family was one of the ones who sold grain out of our house in order to survive. There also was a single restaurant that still operated. It was the place in the little town; there wasn't much else in the way of entertainment. I can't remember what it was called, but I can still picture where it stood and the Muslim man who ran it—his name was Ahmed, and he was very kind to me and the other children who visited. However, we didn't visit often.

At the end of the summer each year, my mother would hire a couple of ladies for a week or two to help her prepare the food that we would survive on for the winter months. They worked tirelessly down in the basement, preparing a variety of foods. Vegetables—eggplant, cucumber, squash, every imaginable thing—were kept preserved in huge jars. The women also gathered several hundred kilos of olives from nearby olive groves, which they turned into olive oil. Each batch was prepared a different way so that we had a variety of flavors. They also made butter, but it was a much different version than we have here in America. It was very concentrated—they'd boil the impurities out—so that it would last longer.

The things we subsisted on most, though, were the things that lasted longest. The ladies made a form of dry yogurt that could last for an entire year. They prepared meats, mostly lamb, with fat and salt that lasted between six and eight months. The potatoes that grew up in Mount Hermon could store about six months without rotting. And, of course, the grain that came from our land was ground up and lasted for the entire year as well. It was with those grains that the helpers prepared our bread, which was the biggest part of our diet.

The biggest meal of the day was lunch. For dinner we'd eat olives or cheese or vegetables. Summer eating was the best because the vegetables were fresh, and you could feast on all kinds of fruits—grapes, plums, apples. But no matter the time of year, we always had enough to eat.

Other provisions came by camelback from Palestine. Palestine wasn't really that far—I could see Israel from our balcony. There was a lot of traffic coming through that way, not just on camelback but on horses, too, which were the more common mode of transportation. These animals were fascinating to me, and I wanted to ride them very badly. So I did.

When people came through town on their horses, they usually tied them down while they rested or had a meal. When I saw someone passing by, I'd follow them and wait around for the owners to leave. As soon as they were gone, I untied the horse and rode it for a while until the owner came back. It was a thrill to me, but it was something that my father, and George for that matter, looked down on very much. I anticipated receiving punishment, and I nearly always received it, but it didn't matter. It was worth it. I wanted to do everything. I probably rode every horse that ever came through.

I used to do the same thing with camels. Some of the people riding camels came from Palestine, and they were captivating to me as a boy. I mean, we weren't living in a modern society, but these people lived out in the open. I visited with them, and they seemed to like me because I was an active little boy. But little did they know that when they took a nap, I'd borrow their camels right from under their noses.

I had other adventures, too. One of my brothers-in-law, Amil Shdeed, was a general practitioner for the people in my town and in the area around it. It really is amazing that he was able to do so much with so little. He took his profession seriously and read every book about diseases that he could get his hands on. There wasn't much available in the way of medicine or medical equipment, but he managed to help a lot of people and save a lot of lives. I used to tag along with him sometimes when he made his rounds, mostly because he drove a Jeep from town to town and I wanted a ride in the car. But I also had a curiosity for what medicine was like. Maybe I was subconsciously preparing for what would be my calling later in life. Either way, I had a great time with him, riding around and watching him do his work.

We didn't always get along so well, though; it took me a while to warm up to him. We were very close as a family, and I depended on my older siblings a lot. They doted on me, and I took advantage of their kindness. So when my sister decided it was time to be married, I did not want her to leave the family! We threw her a big wedding party, which the whole community got involved in, but the entire time I refused to call her "the bride." I didn't want my life to change. But I grew to love and appreciate her husband.

Life was intriguing. I enjoyed every second of it. I was carefree as a child and I couldn't have asked for a better playground than Marjeyoun. But my life wasn't always the charming account you might expect in a place so picturesque.

Chapter 2: The War

You could hear the bombs from our home. They shattered the earth as they rained down from the sky. At a young age, the town where we lived was ravaged by war. If you used your imagination, you might have thought that the lights and the sounds were just a thunderstorm. When the bombings grew closer, though, it became apparent that our little town would have to evacuate.

We were a colony of France, so when French fell to Hitler, so did Lebanon. While we were technically under Vichy rule, the government was really controlled by the Nazis. Lebanon was hotly contested between Germany and the Allies, and it became a battlefield. And so one morning, while the rest of my siblings and my father climbed onto donkeys, mules, and camels with our meager supplies to travel to the near town of Kworhouna, I climbed into a cart with my mother. I was upset that I was too small to ride a donkey. I'd always been drawn to animals and had a great desire to ride them. My feelings occupied me during the whole trip, and now the only other detail I can remember is that halfway through the journey, we had to get out and walk. The load was too heavy for the device to get us all the way up the hill.

We rented another house in Kworhouna and survived for a few months on the wheat, oil, and lentils that we had brought with us. It was barebones living, enough to make it seem as though living in Marjeyoun was fit for royalty. There wasn't much we could do to help ourselves there, since our situation was precarious. The war followed us to that little town, too, and there was no escaping it the second time. You could hear bombs exploding in the distance once again.

Luckily, none of us were hurt during the w
the Allies came and attempted to free the peo,
government. It was mostly Australian and Moro
who came. They tried to build bridges and
infrastructure, but they were really just throwing
around.

I discovered when I was older that the war wasn't eve..
supposed to come to Southern Lebanon. It was supposed to
look real, but it wasn't supposed to be real. And to that point,
that was our experience. It certainly sounded real, but we were
at a distance, and it only had minimal effect on my family. We
hadn't seen or experienced it for ourselves. It seemed make
believe.

But then we returned to Marjeyoun.

No one had been around to clean up after the war. There
were dead soldiers and dead mules strewn every which way,
some of them half-buried in the dirt. To this day, I still picture
feet sticking up from the ground. But that wasn't all. There
were casings, too. Empty explosive shells and gunpowder and
all sorts of things I'd never seen, or touched, before. And
curiosity got the best of me.

Against my—and, of course, my mother's—better judgment,
I decided it would be fun to go and explore among the dead
bodies. When my parents didn't know what I was up to, I
scoured the battlefield, playing amongst the dead bodies and
collecting pieces of exploded bombs. It's by the grace of God
alone that I didn't die doing so. But, God did give me a slap on
the wrist. I developed an infection.

Knowing what I know now, I realize that that infection put
me much closer to death than I've ever been in my life. I had an
abscess in my groin right over a major artery. There were no
antibiotics. And there was no anesthesia. Four guys had to hold
me down—I remember that part of it very well; I was just a
young boy, why did they need so many men to hold me
down?—and Amil just nicked it, miraculously removing it. If
he'd gone just a little deeper, if he'd hit that major artery, there

been nothing he could have done to save me.

..er, less intense, result of the war is that we lost our
Bible, and so I'm not entirely certain when my birthday
ou see, in Lebanon, there was no real rush to get a birth
ertificate like there is in America (where you walk out of the
hospital with one). Instead, tradition is to write down the
details a year or two later in the family Bible. I've been told
that I was born December 7, 1931, but there's no real way of
being certain of that. Something I am certain of, though, is that I
was about four years younger than the next youngest child in
the family. Owing to the fact that each of my other siblings
were about two years apart in age, I'm pretty sure that I was a
mistake.

Knowing when I was born wouldn't have mattered, anyway,
because we don't celebrate birthdays. When you live in a place
where having a small shelter and enough food to get by is
considered middle-class, you don't have many resources, or
desire really, to celebrate "trivial" things like the day you were
born.

In order to gain a little bit more wealth, my father sold our
family's land in Palestine. It was a big chunk of land that had
been in the family for generations. It was very fertile, and it
was how we were making a living. Unfortunately, it didn't
produce as much as it could have because lots of crops were
being stolen. So Father decided to take a risk, and he sold his
portion of the land.

There were three other families who owned portions of the
land as well. They didn't want to sell their portions because it
would have had to be split between them and their relatives,
leaving a very small profit for themselves. When they found out
my father sold his share of the land, they were angry. He did a
very good job taking care of the land, and since he was
respected in the community, he got a lot of other people to
come and help protect him, too. The crops would suffer
without his help.

When they found out my father sold his share of the land to
Israelis, they were even angrier. My father didn't care who the

land was sold to. He thought that Jews were just as good as Christians or Muslims, so it didn't bother him one bit to sell a bit of land to the Jews. But it got him in a lot of trouble with Al-Kaf, or the Black Gloves. My parents tried to shield me from what was going on, but I picked up on things. And it was hard to miss that there was an attempt on my father's life.

My father was smart and well connected and he knew how to get around in the government, so he had a lot of friends. When our friends and relatives heard that Al-Kaf was after my father, they immediately came to his aid. We had a nice house, but the door was never locked. Instead, we used the second floor as an extra security measure. We placed men up there with big, heavy rocks to use on any intruders.

They couldn't use guns at that time because under French rule, if you were caught with a handgun you rotted in jail. If you wanted to hunt, you used a small gun that you put your own powder in. It wasn't good for anything but shooting small birds, like quail. There were very strong restrictions. The only people who owned guns besides convicts were four or five soldiers on horseback who controlled the whole county.

But our helpers didn't need guns. These rocks really could do the job anyway. They were the kind of rocks that were used to compact the roofs on some of the clay houses in the area. And ultimately, the risk of being clubbed to death by a rock was not one that the assassins wanted to take. After a few months of supporters keeping watch over our front door, my father's life was spared and the danger passed.

Despite all the negatives that came from selling that land, it turns out my father had tremendous foresight in doing so. Not only did his partners lose their share in the land a few years later during military conflict (and they received nothing for it), but my father paved the way for my brother and I to improve our and our families lives forever, through gaining a good education.

Chapter 3: Early Education

I disliked school as a child.

Many people probably can, and do, say the exact same thing, but most of them don't have the experience I did. As a young child, I attended an Orthodox Christian school that was taught in French. I didn't enjoy it; it wasn't fun. I don't mean to say that it was boring—in fact, I've always enjoyed learning and the subjects in school never put me to sleep. But it was strict, and I didn't like the rules.

Whenever an adult walked in, the students were expected to stand. You didn't sit again until you were instructed to do so. You were supposed to behave just like you did at home—children were meant to be seen but not heard (unless you were called on). And if you broke any of the school rules—for instance, talking back to a teacher—you were punished physically. Sometimes they'd make you kneel for long periods of time or they'd have you stand in the corner with books in your hands and your arms straight out. The teachers could be very creative with their punishments. The head of the school, though, was not as creative. He administered good, old-fashioned spankings. That's about the only thing I remember about the man besides the fact that he had an unusually red beard.

My oldest brother, Fayez (born third in the family), was one of the teachers there. I was a difficult student, so I got more punishments than average, most often at his hand. He watched my behavior carefully and he took excessive liberties in punishing me. Because he was my brother, he could get away with it. I don't think that's why he punished me extra, though. I believe he truly cared about my education and wanted me to take it seriously. His presence in the classroom affected my behavior and attitude in school. I didn't want the other kids to think that I was getting good grades just because my brother was the teacher. So when I was in classes with him as a teacher, I tried a little harder than I normally would have.

The day started out with a Bible class, which was attended by everyone. I paid little attention; I never was much of a scriptorian or theologian. But since the school was Christian-run, it was mandatory for each student to attend. After Bible class ended, the students split up into the four or five rooms on the first floor of the chancery (the building where the Bishop lived). Generally these classes were split by age and, therefore, skill level. A few of the classes were combined for certain subjects, but it's been so long that I can't remember which subjects they were. For most of the day, though, you were with other students your age or close to it.

The school was small so there weren't many teachers. On the days that I could handle sitting still and following all the rules, I generally enjoyed my teachers. I don't remember any of the lessons they taught, and I don't remember much of my interaction with them. But I will always remember one interaction I had with a grade school teacher of mine.

I remember this teacher's name, but it's difficult to put into English, so we'll just call her Miss. Miss had a vascular malformation, hemangioma (sometimes called a strawberry mark), in one of her cheeks. It was a big one, so her face is hard to forget. But she was memorable for better reasons, too. Miss was a great teacher. I had great admiration and respect for her. But during this one interaction, she did something that really bothered me.

On this particular day, I was wearing a piece of clothing that was handed all the way down from my oldest brother to me, a green long-sleeved jacket. A lot of my clothes were hand-me-downs, but that was probably for the best. Even a decent garment wouldn't last long thanks to my active nature. By the time my clothes got to me, they were rags, especially this green jacket

I didn't really care much or pay attention to the clothes I was wearing, so I didn't feel bad about wearing this jacket to school. However, Miss noticed and she cared. During Bible class, she made a big fuss of the whole thing to the entire class. Only, I wasn't the one she blamed. Violette, my sister who was born sixth, was the one who got reprimanded. In front of the whole school in this little classroom, the teacher sternly told my sister how ashamed she was of her to allow her brother to have holes in the elbows of his jacket and to come to class that way. There's no way that Miss could have known that the jacket had been repaired so many times that it was probably beyond repair.

My family was always considered middle class, or at least those are the airs my father gave. We were respectable people, and we were prosperous (at least in comparison to other families in the area). But were prosperous because we had a lot of land, not because we had decent cash flow. If I couldn't afford a pair of sandals that cost a dollar, how were we supposed to be able to afford to buy me a new jacket?

Besides all that, why was Violette the one being blamed? It wasn't as if she had much control over me. I was a very active boy. Clothes stood no chance against my energy and games. Even my shoes wore out quickly. The only one who had any effect on my behavior was my mother. If Miss should have been singling anyone out, it should have been me.

But more than anything else, it bothered me that Miss had decided to deal with the issue in public. I wasn't even the one she was embarrassing and I felt bad. It really bothered me that she would do something like that to my sister.

Because of incidents like this, because of the discipline of the school, and because I had a hard time satisfying my curious and energetic nature in such a limited classroom, there were a lot of days when I would ask permission to go to the bathroom and then never came back.

Altogether, I think I probably missed a year or two worth of classes. As a result, my teachers and peers lost confidence in me. They thought that I should be sent to go work the farm instead of being educated. "Let him toil away," they said; it would be the only thing I would be good for anyway. I was a bad student, and I was quickly falling behind the others my age.

It was my mother who helped make up the difference. She was the one who believed in me. She was my cheerleader. She helped me with my schoolwork when I wasn't in school, and she encouraged me to learn my alphabet by rewarding me if I sat through a lesson with her. But it took a lot of coaxing from mother to convince me to go back to school, so in the meantime when she wasn't helping me with lessons, she encouraged me to help her with the chores.

I looked up to my mother very much and I wanted to do everything I could to please her. I was complimented that she would even want me to help her. She often gave me small amounts of money, a piaster or two (worth less than a penny), for helping to accomplish tasks, but I cared more about making her happy than I cared about any sort of compensation for myself. I liked helping mother—although I'm sure I got in her way sometimes, especially when I was younger—so I did a lot of chores around the house and on our property to make her happy.

We had a rather large garden, and it took a lot of time and a lot of hands to maintain it. So when mother encouraged me to help her in it, I gladly accepted. I liked to play in the dirt, anyway. Along with tending the actual plants, she also needed a fence built around the garden. In our little town, fences were built out of rocks. Lots and lots of big, heavy rocks. It took a few weeks, but I managed to haul enough to build the fence that mother wanted. And she was pleased with it.

Also, when I was old enough, and big enough, I got to help prepare the wheat each year during our food preparation. The ladies boiled and dried the wheat, which then needed to be taken to the mill to prepare a portion for cooking and a portion for tabbouleh, which requires a special kind of prepared wheat.

I got to pack the wheat onto a donkey and take it to a mill to have it ground and otherwise prepared. And when it was finished, I got to go and pick it up. This was a real treat to me. It could hardly even be called a chore, because I loved riding the donkey.

I got to do other chores that involved riding a donkey, as well. We got our figs and grapes from a vineyard that was a long distance over big hills. Only a mule or donkey could navigate it safely. Looking back I wonder how my family could possibly have let me done that by myself.

We borrowed a donkey from one of the surrounding Muslim neighbors, as we did not have one ourselves. When I first started these chores I was little enough that I'd have to line the donkey with the rock fence to get on. I jumped off of the fence onto the donkey's back. If I fell off of the donkey during the trip, that's tough. I would have to find something else to climb to get back on.

One of the other chores Mother put me in charge of was going to the hen house to collect the eggs each morning. It was the one chore I took real advantage of. We had a lot of chickens, and there was no way Mother could know how many eggs the hens had laid the night before and it was easy to sneak a few out. So, when I was feeling particularly mischievous or had a sweet tooth, I would take a couple to barter in town. I knew it was against mother's rules, and it surely would have gotten me into a lot of trouble if I'd ever been caught.

Like I said before, availability of goods in our little village was practically nonexistent during the Great Depression. But there was still one shop in town that sold sweets, and the restaurant made ice cream, albeit in a very old fashioned way. Depending on my hankerings and the heat of the day, I'd take those eggs straight over to one or the other and get myself a little treat. Mother never even knew, at least that is what I thought.

I soon realized that the thing that would please Mother most was going back to school and being a good student. So I committed myself to studying and made a diligent effort to make up for what I'd missed in my classes. At first, I was placed in classes with the younger children. They were all a lot smaller than me, since I was a couple of years older. It was a little weird at first, but it didn't last very long. They let you skip classes if you were a good enough student, and I was a very bright kid at a very low level.

I ended up skipping a few grades. Eventually I not only caught up to the children my age but I passed them. After attending class for a few weeks, I took a placement test, which landed me in the same class as George, in future years, even though he was about four years my elder. And it was all due to my mother's instruction. Because of her, I eventually finished grade school and was awarded my very own certificate, all in French.

My mother was my cheerleader, and I got along with her very, very well. She was the only person in the world who could control me when I was an active youth. She was truly an unbelievable woman. Not only did she rear eight children (and in a tiny house without running water or electricity), but she managed to keep them happy and alive in an area filled to the brim with endemic diseases. Typhoid fever, tuberculosis, polio, malaria—you name it, we had it. But none of the children caught it (except for me, but we'll talk about that in a little while). Thank God for mothers. I think our survival depended on her.

A lot of the reason we kept healthy was because of how stringent she was about cleanliness. She was as tough as a master sergeant. Everything had to be clean all the time, so things were being washed quite often. You took your shoes off before coming in the house. If you were dirty, you didn't come in the house at all. You washed up before dinner. In cleanliness and every other aspect of home life, you behaved. As a child you were supposed to be seen and not heard. And if you acted up, you dealt with Father.

My father was the real punisher. Being the over-active little boy that I was, I got a lot of spankings from him. And I mean real, good spankings. They didn't hurt me one bit, but they sure did get the message across. My mother had to intervene a time or two when my father got carried away.

Looking back, I'm glad that my father cared enough about my future to use discipline on me. He and my mother were a great team, and it was because of them that I knew structure and discipline as a young boy. Although I was mischievous, I knew the consequences of bad behavior and developed a very strong sense of right and wrong. There is no way I could live in Lebanon now, although it's a beautiful country, because there is no law and order. To me that makes all the difference. The dichotomy that exists between ghettos and Paradise Valley living is very simple: the failure of the family. If you have no family, you have no direction.

When I misbehaved at school, the punishment at school was minimal. It is what I got when I got home that really mattered. There was a code of behavior and ethics, a structure—a father that you respected (and at times feared, but that's okay). It was because of my home life that I became the person that I am today and that I was able to succeed.

My father was a very good man, but he exhibited little emotion. That wasn't necessarily uncommon in our culture. As a man, you aren't supposed to cry or show your weak side. And to some, love can be seen as weak, an emotion to be concealed. I remember that when he'd return after two or three months from inspecting the family land in Palestine we kissed his hand. That was the extent of affection we showed toward each other.

Our father cared a lot for our wellbeing, though, and in turn we had a lot of respect for him. We lived in a very patriarchal society, one in which the father's word was law. If he asked you to do something, you did it, no questions asked. And if he turned down a request, you didn't backtalk to try to negotiate. His answer was final. You couldn't negotiate with Dad. There was no discussion, only listening. You always carried out his wishes. You may grumble against some of his decisions, but you did so silently.

Having learned this lesson the hard way, I took it seriously when my father sat George and me down one day and told us

20

something that would shape our lives for decades to come. "You boys are going to be doctors," he said. He expected great things from his two youngest sons. As if to show us that he was serious, he informed us that he had sold some of his land in Golan Heights to afford to send us to private schools. He had decided that education would be the most important thing in our young lives. He'd also had the great foresight to see that English would surpass French as a worldwide language, so he had signed us up for an English-speaking private school in Aley, called, if my memory serves me right, the National College of Aley.

George and I didn't know a lick of English, so the summer before our new term would start, my father hired a tutor for us, Mr. Homsey, who was a professor at the American University of Beirut. He came five days a week. He was a good tutor, or at least he would have been had George and I been more invested in learning the language. We had no idea the difficulties we were in store for.

I was about fourteen years old when my family made preparations and sent George and me to the private school in Aley. It was beautiful there. Beirut is on the seashore, where it's very warm and humid. But Aley was near the mountains, which were very steep and seemed to be always cool. If you wanted to, you could have almost gone skiing and swimming in the same season, thanks to the different climates. It was a wonderful place to live.

Selling the family land gave my father enough money to move the rest of the family with us. They found an apartment only twenty miles from the school. It was a real upgrade—they had running water by this time even in Marjeyoun. Although they lived close, they never did come to visit. There was no handholding when it came to boarding schools. If you were in school, you were in school—no matter how close by your family lived. As a result, the only time I went to see them was for Christmas and summer vacation. On the other hand, George and I started spending a lot of time with each other for the first time. It was the beginning of a very strong relationship that would last us for the rest of our lives.

My father did come and check on us maybe once a year. He would give us a little bit of money, since my father was always generous that way, but we didn't really need it. The school provided everything the students needed. A little extra cash didn't hurt, though. There was a tiny shack near the school that sold sausage; you could buy a link for a quarter of a lira, which is Lebanon's old currency. (Most everyone uses dollars now.) But that was really all the attention my parents gave us while we were away.

At this time, my parents' grandchildren were taking center stage, anyway. All of the children were growing up and leaving home; I was the youngest and one of the last ones to go. A few of my siblings were considerably older than I was and already had a few children who were only a few years younger than I was. My father spent a lot of time with them and was much more loving to them than he was to his own children, including me. I was just in the way! Grandkids were far more important. I was envious of their relationship. But that's life.

Selling the land in Palestine and moving the family turned out to be a lifesaver. Their new apartment was in the best location in Beirut. It was a nice building—six stories split into two sections, forming twelve apartments and a penthouse—and my father was able to maintain a slightly better income there. It allowed them to upgrade a little in life, especially since they owned the entire building.

We had a "caste" system with no social mobility. You died the same class you were born into, despite any wealth you might have come into along the way. If you weren't born into an influential family, that's too bad. You didn't get any of the perks that came with it. You couldn't work your way up to it. And often, you and your family stayed at the same level of education for generations. That was then, but it gradually changed and upward mobility is real now.

George had a buddy who was the son of one of the influential men in Lebanon. He had firsthand experience with this corrupt system. People would come to his buddy's father and ask "Why don't you open schools for us?" And his answer was always the same. "Why would you need them? My son is going to school, and that's all we need."

So we were lucky to have the means to send George and I, who were only middle class, to an English-speaking boarding school. It wasn't the average Lebanese opportunity, and it opened the door for the rest of our future.

In some ways, attending a boarding school in Lebanon was like attending a military school in America. We didn't wear uniforms, but we were expected to wear decent clothes. Discipline was critical. We weren't allowed outside of campus except for Sundays. On Sundays we were allowed to go to church and maybe go watch a movie or something with our friends. But no matter what we did, we had to be back by six o'clock in the evening. As a senior, though, we really got our freedom. We were allowed out on Saturdays as well as Sundays!

That wasn't the only strict aspect of the school, though. Meals were set on weekdays, and there was no variety. Tuesday's meal was the same every Tuesday, Wednesday's meal was the same every Wednesday, you get the picture. We got great big portions of whatever we were eating that day, for instance beans or wheat. It wasn't always the best-tasting food, but we ate plenty. And mealtimes also didn't budge. If you wanted to eat, you had to be there right on time—we didn't just get to eat when you felt like it. We ate when the bell rang.

Like with the food, there were no options when it came to class schedules. We started at 8 in the morning and ended at 3 or 4 in the afternoon and we all studied the same things as everyone else, which was everything. And at night, it was no different. Everyone had a two-hour study period, and there were no exceptions. You had better sit there and study—or at least pretend to study. If you weren't studying and you were caught, punishment was swift and sure. Discipline was critical for keeping so many boys in line.

Of course, boys weren't the only ones who attended the boarding school, but at times it felt like they were. There weren't many girls, and the ones who were there were isolated and protected. The school was very traditional that way. Since it was a boarding school, the girls were separated from us in an entirely different building for lodgings. And there was absolutely no dating allowed.

Lebanon generally had a very closed society. Women back then were expected to get married, not to be educated. It was irrelevant for them at that time and in that place in the past. Even my parents, who valued education, didn't overindulge on my sisters' educations. With eight children to provide for, my father didn't have the funds. He sent a couple of the girls to a junior college, but that was it. (On the other hand, every one of my kids is very highly educated. I value education a great deal, and luckily I have no problem paying for it.)

But even when getting married, women didn't have much freedom. If Dad didn't like the guy the girl had chosen, the relationship ended right there, no discussion. If Dad did like the guy, he allowed him to come and visit her, but only as long as the rest of your family was there visiting, too. After the couple was engaged, the girl was allowed take a walk with her fiancé down the boulevard, just the two of them, but that's about as private as it got. I never dated at all in Lebanon. In grade school, I had a "girlfriend," but the closest I ever came to her was renting a bike and riding by her house.

But anyway, the students at the boarding school, male and female alike, came from many different countries—Iraq, Saudi Arabia, Syria, Jordan. But they weren't all young. Some of them were old men in the class with little guys. But since the school covered such a large area geographically, only the best students attended. You really had to apply yourself if you were going to be a good student.

The restrictions of the school were easy to deal with in comparison to the content of the classes. Learning English was painful. Arabic is my native language; it's what we spoke at home. In public, Lebanon being a French colony, everyone spoke French. And now suddenly I was taking every subject in English—aside from language classes (French and Arabic), which were in their respective languages—and my English was very poor. It made classes difficult, it made studying difficult, and it was a shock to be immersed into the language that way. I remember crying many nights.

Mr. Homsey had been a decent tutor, but what we'd learned under his tutelage in no way prepared us for the immersive nature of the boarding school. Not only were the classes beginning to get a little more focused and a little harder, but we were learning them in a language we'd never used until a few months before.

Nonetheless, my concentration in school was to do well. It was very important to me to please my parents. In order to be the doctors our father wanted us to be, it was necessary that George and I make good grades. It took me a year or two, but once I had a grasp of the language, I worked very hard until I was once again at the top of the class. I was nearly always second place, but the guy who always somehow managed to beat me to the top spot was my best friend, so I didn't mind very much. I remember that he was from the South, a Shi'ite Muslim. We almost got arrested together while demonstrating against the partitioning of Palestine in 1948, my senior year of high school. He went on to join parliament, moving to the Ivory Coast and becoming very rich.

When I wasn't studying, I spent most of my time on physical activities. I was still pretty macho, and I felt a need to keep in shape. I spent hours and hours during school on campus playing ping pong—I got really good at ping pong—and exercising. I also played soccer with George. Playing it there was different than playing it here, though. When we played, you didn't sub—you played the whole two hours straight, no intermission. If you got injured, your loss. The team just did without you. You really had to work hard if you wanted to do a good job. George and I worked hard and did well. We played on the top team and ended up traveling from one school to another for games.

The only thing that really got me down during high school was the year or so that I was really, really sick. Just as I liked to do in Marjeyoun, I explored as much of the land as I could. The surrounding area had lots of natural fountains and running water, so it had its fair share of mosquitos. Playing near the swamp areas was something our mother warned us not to do (she was a smart lady and had a good sense for protecting her children from the elements) and something George didn't particularly care for. But I did it anyway. My mother also admonished us to cover ourselves with our mosquito nets as we slept, but the mesh bothered me. My siblings all dutifully slept under theirs. I didn't.

It was because of this disregard for the rules that I was the only child in the family to catch malaria. It happened about my second year in high school.

When you contract malaria, you are really very sick. Your temperature skyrockets to around 104. You shake a lot and you feel weak. I'm not sure if it was my imagination or not, but I swear I could feel the eggs of the parasites maturing in my blood. It really is a nasty disease. I had to take medicine for about a year or so to fight it off.

Aside from that, high school was a good time. The restrictions didn't bother me; I had good buddies and I was content. But when it came time to graduate, I was ready to move on.

The graduation ceremony wasn't a big deal. Graduating high school at all wasn't a big deal, to me or to my parents. Sure we were given a diploma and everything, but graduating from such a low level of education didn't mean much. We were going to go on to get much better degrees—our father expected us to become doctors, after all. And being in a culture of non-celebration, high school graduation didn't make the cut for making a big fuss. I mean, if you are going to throw a party to celebrate something as simple as graduating high school, what's left to do when someone gets a law degree or a CPA? Needless to say, none of my family came to my graduation. There were lot of other parents there who made a ruckus when their children's names were called. But it didn't leave a bad taste in my mouth. It was what it was.

I went on to attend the American University of Beirut (AUB). It was a little school that serviced a rather large area geographically. They had a very strict and selective process, so you had to be pretty good to get in. You had to have good grades to go to college in Lebanon. It wasn't an automatic thing like it is now here in America. You had to have a certain standing to get into even its lower division. I was a top student in high school and I still was only just good enough to get in. But that first year, I messed up big time.

At the AUB, you had to declare your track—arts or sciences—at the end of your first year. If you didn't, or if you didn't have the grades to get on the higher track, the university declared for you. You had to have really good grades to get on the sciences track, which was considered the more difficult or higher of the two. If you wanted to get into the AUB's small, but very good and sought after, medical school, you had to be on the science track. That's the one that George and I needed if we were going to go on to become doctors. George had graduated from high school a year before me, so I'd been able to watch him go through his first year at the university. And I'd seen him miss his shot at getting on the sciences track. His grades weren't good enough, and so the university declared him on the arts track. I should have realized from his experience just how hard it was going to be to get where we wanted. That's why I failed.

Instead, I lost focus. I got interested in girls, and I made friends with the wrong people. Instead of studying like I should have been, I was out socializing and getting into trouble. One of my friends was smoking pot—I wasn't; I didn't even know what it was—and he had a car without a license that he wasn't afraid to take out on joy rides. (To be fair, I wasn't afraid to drive it, either. My father's connections to higher ups in the government got me out of a lot of little things.) And so when my time to declare came around, I was also placed on the arts track. I had failed.

Worse than failing, though, was the shame I had to bear when I told my father that I had failed. He had put a lot of money and trust into my and George's education already. It was the only thing he wanted from us, the only thing he really expected. And we had failed him.

But let me tell you now, you learn a lot more from failures than successes. I allowed it to put me off track only for a year. I wasn't about to let that one screw-up keep me from pleasing my father. All George and I wanted to do with our lives was please our parents. So, I made a vow to never let my experience at the AUB repeat itself. But it was a great stumbling block, because my failure meant there was no way I could study in Lebanon to become a doctor. I would have to leave the country. But no matter how hard it would be, I would find another place to study, and this time, I would do it right.

Chapter 4: Trip to America

George and I grew up hearing a lot of great things about America. Not only had we seen all the western movies (which were wonderful, by the way), but we'd heard that there was lots of money to go around there, as well as great schools.

Since George and I both didn't get accepted to study the sciences, we knew that our only path to becoming a doctor at this point was to go out of the country. Since the AUB was very selective of who went on its science path and neither of us had made the cut, we had missed our chance. We wouldn't be able to take any sort of medical classes, or even pre-med classes, in Lebanon. So we decided to head to America. We didn't even care what we would be studying, as long as we got in to a college there. We figured that if we could get a start in petroleum engineering, we would eventually find a way to study medicine somewhere down the line. We'd find a way to go and be doctors. America had all the opportunity I needed. Cowboys, riches, and a great education? What could be better?

My father didn't have the same outlook on the situation as we did. When we came to him practically begging him to let us go, he told us to dream on. I don't think he was very confident that we could make our own way in America. But we were confident.

Or at least I was. George told me that he didn't particularly want to go to America. But he also said that he was open to the idea. If the way was opened for us to go to America to get our educations, he would go with me. He just wasn't as enthusiastic about the prospect as I was. As a result of our deliberations, I applied for both of us to go to an American school.

Little did I know it was very, very difficult applying to American universities. Learning English at the boarding school turned out to be beneficial. I was competing with the cream of the crop. I had to improve my English as much as I could before sending in my applications (my English was not exactly Shakespearean at that point) and I was fortunate to have that foundation.

We sent in our transcripts, but they weren't the best of our class. You have to remember that the AUB had only a small number of students who came from all over the Middle East. They were the best of the best, the creamiest cream of the crop. So George and I weren't even close to being the top students. I was maybe a little better than George was, but not by much.

In the end, our grades were good enough, though. I was accepted at the University of Tulsa, in the engineering program, to begin my sophomore year, and so was George. We were exhilarated at the prospect. All we'd wanted was to get into an American school; it didn't matter what we studied and it definitely didn't matter where.

Except we found out that it did.

When we told Father the good news, he seriously objected to our going to a school in Oklahoma. He told us, "It's West Virginia or nothing." You see, our older sister Violette had moved to West Virginia a year before. She had endured more as an immigrant than any other member of our family had, but luckily she had married a great guy, named Shafeek Ammar, who helped as much as he could with the transition. He was a super gentleman, one of the nicest guys you would ever meet. He was born a Syrian, but he moved to America as a young boy and was legally an American citizen. When he came back to Syria, he met Violette and decided he wanted her as his wife. She married him, uprooted, and moved back to America with him. She was our "in" to America. Father wanted us as close to family as possible, and so the deal was that if we wanted to go to America, we had to be on track to study medicine, and we had to attend a school in West Virginia.

I'm pretty sure that at that time my father thought that West

Virginia was a city. He might have thought differently had he known that West Virginia was much larger than Lebanon. We would be going to a school a couple hundred miles away from Violette. But we weren't about to correct him. It was our one shot to get to America.

We spoke with a few other middle-eastern immigrants who lived in West Virginia, and they agreed to help us get into a school there. We ended up getting accepted into a school in Montgomery, West Virginia, called Morris Harvey. (It doesn't exist as Morris Harvey anymore—now it's the University of Charleston.) At the time, we didn't know how small and insignificant of a school it was, so we were excited to go.

But my father was about to throw another wrench into our plans. "We can only afford to send one of you," he explained. I already knew this. College is and always has been expensive, moving to another country notwithstanding. When we'd gotten the acceptance letters from Tulsa, I'd talked to George and told him that I'd be the one attending. I'd gotten the better grades, and I'd been the one who really wanted to go. He seemed okay with the idea, being less than enthusiastic to go halfway around the world to a foreign country without me. But my father continued, "And George will be the one to do it."

I should have expected it. George was the older sibling. Of course it would be Father's wishes to send the older of the two. But knowing that didn't make me any less angry. After George left on his flight to America, I raised hell. I decided that if I couldn't attend an American University, then I didn't want to advance my education after all. I would just have to find a job someplace, instead. And that place wouldn't be Lebanon. (Lebanon had no jobs, no industry. The only thing it was good for was its good weather and beauty.) Maybe I'd just have to leave the family and go find work on the Persian Gulf.

After two weeks of mild threats, complaining, and attempts at bargaining, my father finally gave in. "Okay," he said with a huff. "I'll send you. But I won't be there to bail you out. You need to straighten out on your own. No skirmishes. No games." I promised him there would be none and the deal was done.

Once Father was convinced it was a good idea, all we had to do was convince America that it was a good idea, too. We had jump through a lot of really strict hoops to get me permission to live there. I had to go through a complete physical exam, including a urine exam, a stool exam, a chest x-ray, and skin tests. I also had to submit an essay to the American embassy proving that I knew a little English. And finally, Father had to submit proof that, if need be, he could support not only me but both George and me for as long as we were in the United States. Once those tasks were completed, I was on my way. The year was 1950.

* * *

The plane was a lot bigger than I thought it would be. I had never seen one before, let alone ridden in one, so I was more than just a little anxious to board the contraption. In fact, it might have been just about the most frightening experience of my life up to that point. And besides that, I was loaded down with quite an ensemble. Besides my regular luggage, I was carrying fresh figs in a basket for my sister and brother-in-law, a thank you from my parents for picking me up from the airport and taking me in. My mother had also made me a half dozen sandwiches to take on the journey, knowing I would get hungry on the way. They were taking residence in my pants pockets, causing them to bulge out the sides a little. And lastly, I had a thousand dollars sewn into my hip pocket.

Sewn in. Meaning that if for some reason I had to actually use the money, I would be taking off my pants somewhere and cutting into them. If the other aspects of the journey weren't harrowing enough, that certainly caused a little extra stress.

It was actually the result of a kindness done by my mother. Before we'd come to the airport, my Father had updated me on my financial status and responsibilities. "We opened a Chase–Manhattan account for you. Here's a checkbook. Don't lose it." I looked down at the small book in my hands, flipping through its pages. I'd never seen a check before. I had absolutely no clue how to use one. But I accepted my father's offering, anxious to keep in his good graces all the way up until the plane took off.

But mother had heard him, too, and she was concerned. "What?" she asked with that concerned-yet-reprimanding tone only mothers learn to master. "Are you sending this boy without any money?"

"He has money in the bank."

"That's not how my boy is going to America. You go and get him a thousand dollars, and I'll put it in his hip pocket. I want to make sure he has money."

And then suddenly I was boarding an airplane with sandwiches in my pockets, a basket in my hands, and money sewn into my clothes. I don't really remember the flight—how long it took, if there was much turbulence, or where I sat on the plane. It must have been relatively smooth, and it was much less intimidating than getting on the plane had been.

When I got off the plane in New York, though, I definitely experienced culture shock. Suddenly there was a diversity of race. Asians here, Hispanics there, and blacks just across the way. And they were all speaking English, so quickly that I couldn't catch a single word of what limited English I might have known. People were bustling here and there and it was all so loud. There were people who seemed to be yelling on the loudspeaker. It was a lot to take in all at once.

The first thing they did was take my figs away. At the time, I didn't understand why they had done it, but there was nothing I could do to stop them. I was very sad, but I also didn't have much time to dwell on it. I had another plane to catch and I needed to figure out where I was going.

My father had given me a phone number to call in case I needed some help navigating my way once I got to America. Perhaps he wrote the phone number down wrong or forgot the area code, I'm not sure, but either way it didn't work. So I took turns wandering around and sitting around the airport, clueless as to where to go.

After a while, I finally stopped a guy who looked like he might be the captain of an airplane. I approached him and, knowing I couldn't rely too much on my broken English, I showed him my plane tickets. He was very kind to me and immediately came to my rescue. After looking at the papers in my hand, he told me that I was in the wrong airport. I'd come in on an international flight, but I wanted to go to Charleston, West Virginia, which was a local flight. I'd need to get a cab to get there.

Now that I knew where I needed to go, I left the airport and found a cab. I don't remember the details of how long it took, what my cabbie was like, or even how much it cost. I had no idea how American currency worked, so when the cabbie asked to be paid, I just took out a few bills and said, "Here's some money." Whether or not it was anywhere close to the proper amount, the man took it.

Once again I was lost inside a busy airport. But luckily, I met a lot of really good people who helped to guide me in the right direction and get me where I needed to go. The entire day had taken longer than it should have, and it had gotten dark a little while before. When I finally found the right people to talk to, they told me that I'd make it to the gate of that last flight to Charleston that night, but only if I hustled.

I ran, but I couldn't see the signs and I wasn't sure where the gate was. I wasn't sure where I was. Taking precious time, I stopped a man and told him what I needed. Seeing that I was mildly distressed and in a hurry, he ran with me all the way to the gate. If it weren't for him, I wouldn't have caught the airplane in time.

As I boarded the plane, tired and out of breath, I felt only a little relief. I was consumed with worry. What if Violette wasn't at the airport to pick me up when I landed? If she wasn't there, I wouldn't have any idea what to do. I was coming in much later than we'd both expected. What if they'd gotten tired and gone home? These thoughts and questions occupied my mind the entire flight to Charleston, so I don't remember much of that flight either.

Luckily, Violette, Shafeek, and George were waiting for me at the gate when I landed. I don't think I'd ever been so happy to see them. After talking to them, I learned that they'd been waiting for hours (most of the day, in fact), but had eventually left the airport and come back to catch the last plane coming in from New York.

The trip from the airport to Violette's house is just as fuzzy a memory as the plane ride and taxi drive had been. But I do remember the houses. I was shocked that the houses there were made of wood and not brick or stone. Were the people here too poor to afford homes like the one he'd just left in Lebanon? I wondered about my new life in a new country and tried not to doze off too much so I'd be able to sleep when we made it back to the house.

And I did sleep well that night, tired from the journey. Good thing, too, because I needed it. I had a lot of catching up to do.

* * *

By the time I convinced my father to let me come and I actually made it to West Virginia, school had already been going for a couple of weeks. I arrived on August 24, 1950. I was excited to continue my education in America.

But when I got to Morris Harvey, boy was I disappointed. I hadn't really known what to expect. George hadn't told me anything about the school in the two weeks he attended or on the way back home from the airport. He'd had a "so be it" attitude about coming to America, and the same could be said toward his attitude toward Morris Harvey. But when I saw it for the first time, there was no deal. It was a Nothing University.

"I don't want to go here," I said to George and Violette after my first day at the school. "I'd rather go back to Lebanon."

They asked me what I wanted from my university. And I told them—I wanted something bigger. Morris Harvey was tiny; it didn't have any choices. There weren't any opportunities in the school, and there sure weren't going to be any opportunities out of it. They understood my concerns and assured me that they'd help me get into West Virginia University (WVU). I did a little research this time, and found that it was better suited to my needs. I was ready to go for it.

We needed some help getting in, though. Not only was it a better school than Morris Harvey, but classes had already started and we hadn't even been accepted into their program. Luckily, we had connections to the chairman of the board of the school. His name was Bill Thompson. He was tall and handsome lawyer who was good friends with one of my relatives, William Shdeed, who had preceded George and me as immigrants. My father had helped William and some of his friends and family get to America when they were immigrating, so they were more than delighted to connect us to Bill. He was able to pull a few strings and get both George and me into the school. It was a break that we never expected and could never be more grateful for. We were a couple of weeks behind, but our grades seemed to reflect that we could handle it. It seems I might have even had an academic lead over George even though I was younger.

I'm not quite sure what grade my credits put me at when we started at WVU, but we only had to study there for three years. We had a few credits transfer from the AUB, and I took a French exam that gave me sixteen credit hours. It turns out French was useful for something after all.

* * *

When we first started school, George and I were really foreign. We rented a place together with our "cousins" (distant Lebanese relatives) Floyd Shdeed and Sidney Farha while at WVU, and it was fine for the first few days. George was responsible for managing our money, and I was responsible for making the food. We were unfamiliar with American food, so we usually ended up eating tuna and scrambled eggs. But after a few days, we ran into our first in a series of many cultural conundrums.

We had no idea what to do with our trash.

We knew enough to line our trashcans with bags, but when a bag filled up, we had no idea what to do with it. After we filled up a bag or too, the smell started to be bothersome, so we decided to throw the bags out into the snow-covered lawn of our place. It wasn't long before the Public Health Department came by, informing us that they'd had a complaint from a neighbor. They ordered us to clean up the mess, and the responsibility fell on me because I was the youngest and the other three didn't want to do it. I didn't really mind. We never had to do it again, because after that incident, the Health Department informed us about trash collection services. From then on we learned that the trash man would pick up our bags.

* * *

Not only were the food and customs difficult, but it was difficult living in a place where everyone spoke English. It was challenging to understand conversations with the American boys and girls because they spoke so fast. We weren't used to that.

Adjusting to the coursework especially was difficult since everything was in English. Studying to me meant translating the information into Arabic and then learning and retaining what it all meant. It made taking tests difficult. I'd read the question in English, translate it to Arabic, answer it in Arabic, and then translate it into English. My teachers were generally kind to me about it, though. My chemistry teacher, Dr. Hickman, was especially kind. After taking my first test in his class and timing out, I began to cry, frustrated that I had known the answers but hadn't been quick enough to get them out. Dr. Hickman let me into his office to finish the exam. I ended up getting one hundred percent. I was very grateful to him for allowing me to finish. His actions and the actions of the other teachers at that school were a stark contrast to the styles of teaching I'd been accustomed to in Lebanon. It was the actions of people like him that planted the love for America and its citizens in my heart.

Having experienced failure at the AUB, I focused hard at WVU. After that first year at the AUB, I never allowed myself to earn any grade below a B. I considered a B a misfortune. A C was unacceptable. I only got Bs in classes like sociology or philosophy, where the answer doesn't matter so much as the way you get to it and you need to be able to explain yourself in English. In order to combat more grades like those, I was careful with what I chose as my electives. I took as few Humanities classes as possible, instead preferring courses like calculus or physical chemistry. I took as many science classes as I possibly could. There at least the answers were either right or wrong!

In the meantime, I did everything I could to improve my English. I carried a Reader's Digest with me wherever I went. I read whenever I had a spare moment, and if I didn't know a word, I'd look it up in the dictionary and write it down a few times until I remembered it. Eventually my English was getting along better.

Soon I was high up in the science division. I credit a lot of that to my studying habits, rather than my innate intelligence. I studied harder than anyone I've ever known. I was very compulsive and focused, even to the point that I could summarize the book in each of my classes. While I was studying, I would underline the most important parts of each book, copy them down, and keep those notes in a little folder. That was my study habit, and it's how I not only got through college but got good grades doing it.

George was a good student, too, but his study habit was different. I was very useful to him, not only because I helped him to stay on task but because he always read my folders when exams were coming up. He could be compulsive and focused, too, but he was nowhere near the extent I was. He needed the extra time because he enjoyed a lot of good-looking girlfriends. Girls flocked to him because he was tall and handsome. I, on the other hand, was short and stubby. And I was all business.

That's not to say that I didn't date a lot, though. I had a few lookers back in college. But George took it to the next level. I settled for the dates I got, but even pretty girls weren't good enough for him. No, George was much more cherchez la femme than that. They had to be pretty and popular. And he wouldn't just go for one of the cheerleaders—no, he wanted to date the homecoming queen. (And to his credit, he did.)

But both of us got a lot of dates at WVU. We were a novelty to those girls. Even though our English wasn't that great, there were a lot of things about us that made us stand out against the normal pool of guys. We were exotic. We had accents. We didn't dress like those other guys. We didn't care about football. (I mean, we came to like it eventually. A couple of years living in America and you can't help it. But at the time we didn't care.) So at WVU I still allowed myself to be interested in girls, but this time I balanced it appropriately with my studying.

I also didn't let myself study so hard that I didn't have any time to enjoy my hobbies. At the university, I took up ping pong again. I'd gotten really good during my days at the boarding school, but I was on a whole new level when I started playing with my college-age peers. And this time the stakes were higher—a quarter a game. I made some good money from the games I won there. I was a champion at the ping pong tables.

* * *

Around the end of my second year at the university, I was invited to join Phi Beta Kappa, which is the oldest honor society for the liberal arts and sciences in the United States. When they extended the invitation, I had only one thing to say.

"What is it?"

I'd never even heard of it before. I'm sure I surprised the guy who was contacting me. "It's an honor society," he simply said.

That sounded pretty nice. I didn't understand how big of a deal it was then, or what was involved, and so I said, "That's fine, sign me up."

But he then informed me that if I wanted to participate, I would have to pay first. "It's thirty dollars for the key." I didn't want to pay that kind of money, so I thanked him kindly but told him I had changed my mind.

I didn't think much of the exchange until I was approached by a Lebanese friend of George and mine, named Richard Elias, a few days later. Apparently he was on the Phi Beta Kappa committee. "Jim," Rich exclaimed when he found me studying for my exams. "Are you crazy? You can't turn this down. It's a big honor!" He let me know that not many students were selected. Not even George had made the cut. After hearing him praise the society for a little while, he convinced me to change my mind, albeit begrudgingly. I was mildly proud to be awarded something that seemed so special to so many people, but Gee, you could go to the movies four or five times for thirty dollars!

Clubs and our social lives weren't the only things draining our money. School was expensive in many different aspects and since we couldn't qualify for student loans, George and I knew going in that we wanted to take jobs during our time off in the summer. We knew how strict things could be for us as immigrants. We could take no fewer than twelve credit hours each semester. (That wasn't a problem for me. I graduated with 160 credit hours when the requirement was only 128. We carried over 20 hours each semester because we wanted to finish rapidly.) Every semester we were required to report our grades and our schedules to the immigration department. They also required us to keep them up-to-date with our changes of address, both during the school year and during the summer. So we made sure to start early in obtaining permission for the jobs we did over the summer. We started preparing for that two months before school let out—not only was there a lot of paperwork for us to fill out but we also had to wait for the departments to approve and file it. I wanted to make sure we had permission to work. It was a good thing we did, too, because those summers changed our lives.

Chapter 5: My First All-American Job

When my first summer came around, some of my friends asked me how I was going to spend my break. I told them that I wanted to get a job, because I was costing my parents a lot of money. I wasn't quite sure at that point what I was going to do, but I was sure that I would be able to find something, whether it be on my own or with the help of some family members. They told me there was no need for that—they could hook me up with a job. They were going to Cleveland for the summer to work and I was welcome to come along if I wanted.

"Deal me in," I said. "I'll go."

We stayed in a small, terrible apartment in Little Italy, which at the time was a "war-zone." There was shooting and stabbing nearly every night. And we were just four kids stuck in a room with a couple of bunk beds. But we didn't mind the cramped area; we wanted the experience. And it didn't take long to find work. I got a job with Eaton Manufacturing and started working immediately. The hours weren't great, and since I had to catch two buses to get to work, I had to wake up at 4:30 or 5 in the morning just to make it in on time. I didn't mind, though, because the pay was going to be good, and I enjoyed the physical work. My job was to load and unload Semi trucks.

But one day, there was an accident.

The day had started off normally enough. I was unloading and loading, as usual. Then, during one of my trips, I noticed a corked glass container on a dolly. I'm not entirely sure what it was, but I think it was some sort of acid. I didn't think much of it at the time.

Somehow during the workday, the container hit a ridge, and the cork came off. The liquid spilled down from its perch, right onto the face of one of my coworkers. For a second, I couldn't do anything but watch and feel awful. It had happened to someone I hardly knew, but it was terrible to think that now he might be scarred for life. I was sad for him. But I was also scared. What kind of place is this that something like that could happen? I asked myself. I left right then, without picking up my pay, and I never returned in a very sad condition.

I spent a few days at the apartment with no money and nothing to do. Luckily, George called to check in on me. I told him that I wasn't doing well—I had no money, and I'd quit my job so I wasn't going to see any more money anytime soon. He informed me that he was staying with Ralph Farha and Louise, his wife, was fixing him lunches every day to take to work. He'd found a good job in West Virginia at an Appalachian Power Plant and he could get me in on it, too. The company wanted to expand into the mountains, and they needed more men to cut brushes and dig ditches. He sent me the money for a bus ticket and I went.

Working for the Appalachian Power Plant was one of the best decisions I made during my college career. Not only was it work that both George and I enjoyed doing, but we were making good money doing it. We were very sensitive to the fact that we were depleting our parents' money during the entirety of our secondary education. It's not that our parents ever complained—in fact, all we had to do was ask and my father would send us the money we needed, no matter how much it was. But we were grateful to have their help and didn't want them to suffer from lack of money more than was absolutely necessary to get us through our educations. So we took every opportunity we could to save a little extra money. Any money we saved was money we wouldn't have to ask for from home.

And working for the power plant turned out to be lucrative. The bosses there were kind and generous, and whenever they could find an occasion to, they let us work double shifts. We were paid time-and-a-half for our second shifts. Working double shifts was only mildly tiring—we were young and fit and ready to work. At one time I thought I was making more money than the president of Lebanon made legally.

They put us to work wherever work was needed. If brushes in the mountains needed to be cut, we climbed the mountains to cut brushes. It didn't matter that we were up high in the mountains, where the land was infested with poisonous snakes. We purchased uniforms, hard hats, and boots with a steel safety toe, and that was good enough to keep us from sudden death. If a ditch needed to be dug, we dug ditches. If the trucks needed a driver, we drove trucks. Occasionally we even swept the floors of the building, which was rather large. If we weren't being paid as much as we were, we might have left, but being what it was, we didn't really care where we were put to work or what sort of work we were doing.

After a few weeks of working, George and I made a grave mistake. We had someone take a picture of us in our safety gear and, wanting to keep our parents informed of our activities and to let them see how happy we were, we sent the picture to our parents. We thought it would be harmless, but it turned out that it hurt my father's pride. We came from a respectable upper-middle-class family and he was very upset that we were working as common laborers. Father thought that sort of labor was below us. He was highly regarded in his town. Having his kids work could hurt his reputation, and they say that perception is reality. The culture of Lebanon reinforced his ideals—if you were the station of our family and you needed a shoe repaired, you had a servant carry the shoe to the shoe shop. Labor was just not suited for our class.

He wrote immediately to our distant cousin Saleem Farha saying, "You stop them from working, otherwise I'll withdraw my support and they'll have to leave the U.S."

We wrote back to inform our father that we had quit our jobs per his instructions and that he didn't have to worry about us taking that sort of job again. It was a blatant lie. We didn't mind it and it was good money, so we kept working there until the summer was over. But we never did send home any more pictures.

It wasn't so much that we didn't care about our father's wishes. It was more that we knew the pressure we were putting on him financially, and we wanted to ease the burden as much as we could. It didn't hurt our pride to work for the power plant, and what father didn't know couldn't hurt him. In fact, we were sure we were helping him. Father was always generous with the money he sent to us—he always sent just as much money as we requested. But we knew that as foreigners, our tuition was high, even higher than the average student's. On top of that you had to pay for rent, for food, and anything else you needed to survive. We knew how much we were draining my parents. We knew how hard it was to make money in Lebanon, and what a dollar would buy in Lebanon is far greater than what it would buy in America. In Lebanon, we were upper middle class. In American standards, we would have been low middle class. So we worked to supplement our revenue to decrease our parents' outflow.

We also didn't want to quit our jobs because we had a lot of good times at the power plant. Even if they were sometimes embarrassing. For instance, George and I were scared out of our lives once. When transformers have enough pressure exerted on them, they shoot up a flame-like substance. It's a normal occurrence, and it's not dangerous, but George and I had never seen anything like it before. One day, the first time we noticed it, we thought that the power plant was on fire. We didn't ask any questions or try to warn anyone else, we just booked it out of there. We hopped an especially tall fence and ran all the way down the road to a creek. After a while, when we felt it was safe to come back, we walked back to the main gate's entrance. There were our coworkers, waiting for us and laughing. We'd been the only two workers to get scared and run. They liked to make rude jokes about it after that.

I guess some of our coworkers decided from that experience that it would be easy to pull pranks on us, because we got pranked a lot following the incident with the transformers.

Once, they dumped an entire bucket of water on me while I was climbing the stairs. That got me mad. They were lucky there were so many stairs to climb; otherwise I would have pummeled them when I got to the top.

When we had some downtime, we liked to spend it with the other workers our age. It was a common summer job for college students that year, and so there was quite a group of us. There was a lot of horseplay and a lot of fun. The power plant was near the Kanawha River, so we'd go hang out there sometimes. Some of the boys would take a wheelbarrow and ride in it like a makeshift boat across the river. George and I never did that, though. We didn't swim, and being inside the wheelbarrow was a bit too close to death for us.

Working for the power plant also gave us privileges to shop in the company store, which I bet most of you have never seen the likes of before. It fascinated me. It was owned by my cousin, Saleem. The Union, issued their own money in tokens, or union decals. Most of the currency exchanged was in Union tokens; you took your pay in tokens, and you paid for merchandise from the Company Store in tokens. It was a general store, and it really had anything you would ever need.

The company store was a big deal, probably difficult to manage, and it was run by an uncle, Saleem Farha, who I respected a great deal. He was a smart fellow, the one who got the cousins organized. He wasn't the only Lebanese immigrant who ran a store, though. There were many in that little community, in fact. They sold everything in their stores. For instance, their store in Palton, WV, sold shoes, dresses, cigarettes, and food. Palton was a very minute town, more like a village, really. It had wooden sidewalks, just like the good Old West. The immigrants who ran it did very well for themselves. They had a willingness to work and a fire in their bellies. They became prominent people in tiny communities. In one of the stores near Montgomery, called Shdeed Mercantile, they employed probably one hundred or so others to work for them. But that's just an estimate from my younger years. Things always seem a lot bigger when you are young, and that number might be slightly inflated.

During the summers, we could have stayed with Violette in Oak Hill, but we really didn't need babysitting. We visited her sometimes when we had time off, but not often. There were no middle-eastern communities there, which meant that there really was nothing to do. Violette never went to community activities or parties or anything like that. We liked it better a bit farther south, in Montgomery and Cedar Grove. They were small cities, although not quite as small as Palton, and the people there lived in tiny houses that were impressive to me. A lot of Shdeeds and Farhas lived there, and they took care of us. They were the most generous, hospitable people.

The immigrants weren't the only ones in the community to treat us well. There was a man who you might call a hillbilly who even helped me get to work each day. When I first started working for the power plant, I would hitchhike once in a while to get to work from Montgomery to Cedar Grove. It was only six or seven miles, not far at all to drive but definitely too far to walk. It was a nicer time then, and I wasn't afraid to hitchhike. (There's no way I would hitchhike now. I would be scared to death.) The people in this community were always very kind.

Anyway, one particular day my hillbilly friend picked me up in his pickup. He asked where it was that I worked. When I told him, he informed me that he worked there, too. He asked if I drove a car, and I told him I didn't but that I was willing to pay for him to take me to work every day. He said there wasn't a need for that. "You just stand where I picked you up right after the bridge every morning and I would be happy to give you a ride."

As if that weren't kind enough, he also took me home from work most days (the days when I wasn't working a double shift), even though his shift ended twenty minutes before mine. He also refused to accept any money, even when I offered it. It was him and people like him who made my time in West Virginia so enjoyable. I learned so much from these simple, kind people.

The Lebanese in West Virginia were not only kind, but they

were a lot of fun. When you were with them, you began to transform, to really live. They used to host picnics in a place I'll never forget (and I haven't been there in 50 years): Hawk's Nest. It's a beautiful state park and during the summer, the weather was fantastic. Together, everyone would set up card tables on which the wives would place the food they had prepared beforehand. There was always lots of food. After eating, the guys would play poker while the ladies visited.

That wasn't the only time they played poker. George and I frequently watched our distant Lebanese relatives play the game. Every so often, the winner would give us $10 from their earnings, which at that time was a heck of a lot of money. (That's probably why I love to gamble so much now; I watched them gamble all the time!)

These distant relatives—William Shdeed, Henry Shdeed, Saleem Farha, Ralph Farha, and many others—let us into more than just their picnics and poker games; they let us into their homes and their hearts. They treated us like their own children. They made us feel at home, like a real part of the community. They always offered us food free of charge. And other things, too—whenever we went to a store in need of a handkerchief or a shirt, they'd just give it to us. We lived in their houses like their children—we ate there, they did our laundry, and they really treated me like a son. While George stayed over at Ralph Farha's house, I stayed two summers with Aunt Bahia Shdeed, sharing an extended porch with her son, Floyd. There were two bedrooms in her house, one for her and one for her daughter, Dolores. I had never met them before we came to America, and yet I felt comfortable with that family and the rest of the community. It was incredible.

These people, by American standards, should have been nothing but strangers. They didn't know us and they didn't owe us anything. But they went out of their way to make sure we were taken care of. Aunt Bahia, William Shdeed, and the others in the area were truly magnificent and helpful people.

Sadly, when school started up again, we had to live apart from them. It was this way for our final two years at WVU.

Morgan Town was almost two hundred miles away; it was much too far for us to commute and visit our new friends, so we saw most of them during the summers only. However, we had the opportunity to see at least one of them regularly.

We had an Uncle, Aziz, who was in the wholesale business. He participated in the rotary club in Morgan Town, and he made special efforts to see us. He would drive the entire two hundred miles to come and spend a Saturday with us. He would bring a trunk full of canned food and cigarettes and maybe a little money on the side. He would buy us a meal or take us to rotary with him and then drive all the way back. It was a very big gesture, a very kind thing for him to do. We weren't really his relatives—we shared the same name, but we were so far removed we were probably tenth cousins. During my free time in Montgomery, I also worked for this same uncle driving trucks up the hollow. And when we graduated, he was there, along with several other of our friends from West Virginia.

Those two summers were the best of my life, and those people had a profound effect on me that was never lost during my lifetime. They were simple immigrants who didn't speak high English, but they were so genuine. They were good, helpful people and without them my first few years in America would have been very difficult and very boring.

Chapter 6: A Brief History of Farhas and Shdeeds in America

It is said that those who deny their heritage have no heritage. I, for one, am very proud of my heritage.

"Farha" comes from a woman's first name "Farhana," which means "happiness." The Farhas are a business family by ancient lineage—they emulated the "Phoenicians," who were merchants in the Middle East thousands of years ago. So it makes sense that in modern times many of the Farhas have followed in their footsteps in creating their own little (or sometimes big!) businesses. It's through hard work, discipline, passion, and creativity that my family has been able to see so much success. They don't accept welfare—we usually have a strong enough support system amongst ourselves that we'd never need to—and they don't accept failure.

The businesses always served to fill a need. Most of the immigrants who came to America opened stores in small communities in order to help them fill their potential and grow into larger, more influential, communities. But growth wasn't always the idea—more often what they were looking for was loyalty. If you have loyal customers, you are always going to have a source of income or support, especially when things get rough. And the best way to make loyal customers is to treat them well. Many of the immigrants started as peddlers and progressed to store owners. They extended credit to customers who normally couldn't catch a break, and they were always sure to stick a little something extra into people's orders. That was a sure-fire way to brighten anyone's day.

Each of these immigrants was tough as nails and sweet as

candy. They earned a lot of respect doing what they did, amongst their friends, families, and communities. The Farhas, Shdeeds, Eddys, and other Lebanese families I met in West Virginia and Kansas taught me a lot about life, love, and good business. I will forever be indebted to them. Although often not blood-related, I will always see them as family. They carried me when I couldn't carry myself, and they became the best friends anyone could ever ask for. It is for this reason I call them my Uncles and Aunts, even though we were practically strangers before meeting. It is a sign of respect, rather than an indicator of familial relationship.

And I had a lot of respect for them. Those immigrants had to have a lot of tenacity to make it in America despite their difficulties. I am very sympathetic to the immigrants' plea, but I know how important it is to have those that push the wagon rather than those that ride in the wagon. I know the Farha family, and I know what life was like before they came to America. They had a lot of religious persecution, they were hungry, and they were beaten up by the Turks. But they didn't feel sorry for themselves, and they worked, and they eventually prospered. They didn't know the language, and they had to peddle their way into society. Most of them started off by running a simple stand, which ultimately enlarged to a real store, where they employed hundreds of people, their own families and members of the community alike.

It's amazing to me that a widow with six or seven kids can raise a family and have all the children rise to positions of leadership and business know-how in the community. I came the easy way compared to them, and it was very traumatic for me as a young boy. Some of my trips were just like a dream; I could hardly remember how I got here. It was difficult for me. So I can't imagine what it was like for them, not being able to speak, not having any money. At least I had my parents who sent us money and support.

My father and other Farhas in Lebanon helped many of the Shdeeds and Farhas get into America, but nowhere near as much as they helped themselves. Many times it was a single forerunner in a family who went ahead and settled somewhere in America, and then they'd come back for a brother or sister or cousin and bring their family along, too. Immigrating through Ellis Island could be tricky. One person I knew very well—Raefa Farha of Kansas City—had to spend six months at six years old at Ellis Island because of an eye infection or some other problem that denied them entrance right away.

Often, after a Farha was able to gain a little footing in America he would send money back to the Old Country to support his family there, sometimes in the hope that the rest of the family would be able to come along eventually, too. Marguerite Samara Farha remembers that sometimes that caused trouble. When people back home caught wind that Farhas were making regular payments to their families on the first of each month, they'd go and ransack the Farhas' house, taking any goods and money they could find.

The Farhas moving from Lebanon usually ended up in specific pockets of the country where they had other family members or friends emigrating to. The most common destinations were Peoria, Illinois; Detroit, Michigan; Sherman Texas; Oklahoma City, Oklahoma; Montgomery, West Virginia; and Wichita, Kansas.

It is the family in West Virginia and Wichita who affected my life in a big way. In West Virginia, William Shdeed was the one who helped George and me find a place in WVU. Bahia Shdeed (who was Sam Shdeed's widow) and her children Floyd and Dolores took me in while I was working summers at the power plant. Floyd would sleep with me on the sun porch and Dolores would pamper us. Sam Farha, Ralph Farha, and Buster Farha also made a great effort to keep George and me out of trouble while we stayed in their neighborhood. Each man had a story of his own, each an inspiration in his own right.

Buster Farha sold shoestrings at street corners as young as age six, eventually graduating to newspapers and making deals until he sold enough at high enough cost to make a living out of the endeavor.

Sam Farha came to America with Sam Shdeed at the

vulnerable age of thirteen. They worked for a businessman in West Virginia, and eventually Sam Farha managed three stores in West Virginia—one in the Montgomery vicinity, one in Charleston, and one in Cedar Grove. Sam Shdeed brought other members of the family to America before his death in 1938, so I never met him. But Sam Farha was sort of the leader of the bunch, and he gave George and me anything we could ever want or need. He was always available to us if we needed help.

Ralph Farha worked in a grocery store when he first immigrated to West Virginia in 1938. He let the coal miners purchase items on credit, even when they were on strike. This developed a bond of trust between the men, and ultimately he was very well known for his good name. His family took George in during the summers when we worked around Cedar Grove.

In Wichita, many of the Farhas were referred to as the "West Side Indians." There you had the descendants of Nahima Salamy Farha, who brought her six young children with her to America in 1920. A brother of hers helped her gain entrance into the city, and she immediately sent her children to school to be educated. When they were old enough, each of the men peddled merchandise, living really on only the most basic necessities so that they could mark down their products even lower than established merchants could. They became known for their affordability and their honesty, and they worked hard to maintain a living for themselves. But as hard as money was to come by, they always kept an extra room in the house for company, which came often. They welcomed newly arrived immigrants and helped them to get on their feet starting their own new lives in America.

Her son, Sam Farha, was very smart in the wholesale business. During the Great Depression, he knew what to buy and what to sell, eventually buying a watermelon patch that otherwise would have gone rotten and selling the watermelons and other fruit at affordable prices. He led the family in creating some of the first supermarkets in the West, first called Cut Rate Supermarket and later changing the name to Farha Supermarket.

When Aziz Farha opened his business, F&E Wholesale Company, he counted on the reputation that his family had already garnered in town. Because they had already established themselves as hard-working, trustworthy people, Aziz was able to use his family's influence to open a few small stores of his own. He opened them in Wichita, Kansas, and in Powellton, Beard's Falls, and Robson, West Virginia. He went on to employ many of his cousins, siblings, and nephews, establishing a place for the Farhas in America even more than before. He was a generous man, always giving his own means to people more in need than himself, and he died a somewhat middle class, but respected, man.

It wasn't always all work and no play. In each instance, family and extended family played a big part in social affairs. There were always lots of gatherings, lots of parties, and lots of pictures, even if there wasn't much money to spend on such affairs. Each of the Farhas and Shdeeds also spent a great deal of time and money in helping their family and friends immigrate or make a home in America after they had already immigrated.

Life in a new country was hard. We were often ill-informed and ill-prepared as foreigners. But we were also blinded, concentrating on one thing. The goal was the only thing in our sight. We wanted to succeed. We wanted to do well in our performance. And above all, we didn't want to do anything to disappoint our parents. It was a very strong driving force. And it's what made the Farhas successful in America.

Chapter 7: Medical School

I graduated from WVU with a tremendous grade point average, very nearly a 4.0. I don't remember for sure, but I think I graduated with honors of some sort. My discipline had paid off. George's had too; his grades were good as well, although probably not as good as mine.

But we almost didn't get in to medical school.

When we came to this country, both George and I decided that we weren't going to disappoint our parents. Ever. We had to do very well no matter what. However, each and every medical school that we first applied to rejected our applications, and most of the time they did so without even requesting our transcripts. What were we doing wrong? We had the knowledge, the grades, the funding. Why weren't these schools even considering our applications? We simply couldn't understand it.

As time started ticking, we began a mad scramble to right the situation. We were determined to find a medical school. Even if I had to go to Australia to do it, I would go to a medical school and I would become a doctor. There was no alternative. I wouldn't be able to withstand disappointing my parents if I didn't fulfill their wishes. George was the first to suggest that perhaps we were missing a key piece of knowledge in getting our transcripts accepted. If we were going to understand the problem, George said, maybe we should go and talk to an adviser.

Lucky thing we did, because it didn't take long for our advisor, Dr. Manning, to figure out and explain to us why schools were rejecting us right from the start. Being ignorant foreigners, we didn't know the system and why it was working against us. The problem was that we had been applying to state schools. There was absolutely no way they were going to take us. Running a medical school is expensive, you see, since you need cadavers, labs, and all kinds of equipment. Most of the funding for state schools comes from taxes. That's why state schools don't charge anywhere near the tuition that private schools do. The slots for medical school students cost the government a couple hundred thousand dollars. So they were obligated to take students who came from taxpaying citizens from their state. (It's a bit different now; state schools typically take a certain number of out-of-staters, but they charge them higher tuition.) These schools weren't looking at our applications because not only were we from out of state, we were from out of the country!

Dr. Manning helped to remedy this by giving us a list of private schools, mostly Ivy Leagues, that we could apply to. We went home and narrowed our lists to about six schools each. We both applied to a few of the same schools, wanting to stick together, but we also applied to a few schools independent of each other to make sure we weren't always competing each other for a spot, just in case. I applied to George Washington University, Georgetown, Harvard, and a few others that I can't remember. But I didn't apply to Tulane. So when George got accepted to Tulane and decided that that was where he wanted to go, I rapidly applied as well. When the answer came a few weeks later, it was a no. All the spots had been filled and they couldn't take me.

I had gotten a couple of interview requests from different schools, though: Harvard and George Washington. George Washington scheduled first.

I remember vividly driving from Morgantown to Washington DC. I left in middle of the night so that I could make the hours-long drive without having to spend any money on staying in a hotel. I drove straight through, without taking any stops besides gas. I stopped at a gas station near the school to change into my formalwear and comb my hair. When I looked into the mirror, I immediately decided that for my interview with Harvard I was going to travel by bus and get a hotel for the night. I looked awful. But I did my best to make myself look decent any way I could manage. Then I made my way to the school, to the office of Dean Parks, the first professor of obstetrics, for what was arguably the most important interview of my life.

A word of advice to anyone who is has to interview, especially for something as important as graduate school: don't drive there on no sleep. Not only will you look like a truck hit you, but you will have physical side effects as well. When I walked into the dean's office, I was already shaking from the nerves. But that was nothing compared to the shakes I got once I started trying to impress a complete stranger while running on no sleep. I was sure that I failed the interview—I was too scared and I was too tired. There was no way I could have made a good impression on him.

I don't remember what sorts of questions were asked or what sorts of answers I gave, but I guess I had some sort of impact on Dean Parks. I was accepted at George Washington University, and I immediately wrote to Harvard withdrawing my application.

I went back to West Virginia, driving trucks and working whatever jobs I could find to make a little money before school started. Come fall, I packed up my things, boarded a bus, and went to Washington DC. I was headed to medical school, which was a great relief. Whatever happened, George and I did not want to disappoint our parents. It was the first time in about seven years that I would be away from George for longer than a few weeks at a time. I was a little nervous about being on my own, but I calmed my nerves and I pushed through it.

When I arrived at Washington DC, I had a night to kill before registration, so I took up lodgings for the night near the college. The next morning, other students showed up for registration, and campus was abuzz with excitement. People crowded the sidewalks and hallways, laughing, talking, and hugging. There were some students seeing old friends, and there were others who were making new friends. I didn't really do either. I mostly watched the others socialize. I felt a little out of place. I couldn't quite keep pace with the conversations they were having. It was still a little too quick for me.

As part of registration, though, there were people around who could help you find housing. Someone asked me if I was looking for a room. I told them I was and that I'd prefer to live someplace close to campus. I didn't want to get too far away, but I also didn't want to get too expensive. I ended up in an apartment with three roommates, who I still remember very well, despite my old age.

The first was Larry Carr. He was from California, the son of a doctor. Like his father, he was a smart man—he went on to become a pathologist. He also had a lot more money to spend on school and on entertainment than I did. The next was John Eden, an only child who went on to become an ophthalmologist. He also came from a wealthy family, and he was showered with gifts, including an Oldsmobile. And finally was Sam Boer, who was a close friend of John's who went on to become an ENT specialist. He was tall, about 6'2. All three of them were very smart boys, maybe even smarter than me. But I had developed an effective studying system during my time at WVU, and I worked harder than they did.

Our apartment was on top of a grocery store—a local grocery store in a bad neighborhood. It was the very definition of the ghetto—a mixed neighborhood in Washington DC where, on occasion, you heard fighting, fire alarms, and police sirens, just as you would expect from the movies. That's really how it was there.

But I didn't spend enough time at the apartment to care too much about our living situation. I spent a lot of time on campus rather than at home. When I studied in the library, I studied until the library closed. Medical school classes were much more difficult than the ones I took at WVU. And with my lack of English hindering me, I knew I had a defect. I thought in Arabic, so I had to translate my study material from English to Arabic to be able to comprehend anything. Because of this, I learned very slowly. What English-native students did in an hour, I did in two or three hours. But I was stubborn and I stuck with my studies no matter how long it took.

I thought I was making it along okay until I had my first exam of the semester. It was for Anatomy. I failed it.

After three years of college, it was my first time ever failing in my schoolwork. "This is it," I said to myself when I first saw my grade. "They're going to kick me out." I was in despair. Medical school was going to kick my butt. It was hard for any normal student, but it was especially difficult since English was not my native language. It was a barrier normal students didn't have to face. And it was one I wasn't sure I was going to be able to overcome. After all this hard work to get into medical school, was I going to have to drop out after the first semester?

Over the next few days, though, I heard some grumbling. It turns out that I wasn't the only one who'd failed the test—over sixty percent of the class had. And the highest grade on the test had been a 75 percent. Soon after that revelation, the Dean called the professor and straightened him out. "Now look," I imagined him saying, "We have the cream of the crop here at this school. If no one is doing well on your tests, someone is to blame—and it isn't the students." He asked the professor to offer a retake on the exam and to focus on teaching the class better.

Things in that professor's class suddenly got much better after that. There was an assistant instructor in the anatomy lab to help answer our questions. The professor gave us more instruction. And they redid the exam a few weeks later. The second time around, I got a B-.

Things got a little better for me around that time, too. I'd made friends with a couple of guys, brothers (twins actually), in my Anatomy class. They were John and Leonard Deré. Sons of a railroad worker, they'd both come from humble means like I had. The only way they were able to afford medical school was through student loans. We had a lot in common. They'd developed a good work ethic. They were also good to talk to. We became good friends quickly and, over time, we became the best of friends.

John was single and Leonard was married. They liked me and I loved them. And I loved Leonard's wife. They were some of the best people I'd ever met. They were one of the reasons I did okay at medical school. In fact, I graduated in the top quarter of my class of 125 students, but if it weren't for the Derés, I'm sure I wouldn't have done half as well as I did. They were very smart boys, top of the class, and when I first confided to them that I was struggling with my studies, they offered to help me. I gratefully accepted.

And it truly was a struggle for me the first year of medical school. I really had to depend on the Derés to get through. As with other disciplines, there are a lot of lectures in medical school. The Deré boys always gave me carbon copies of the lectures, which helped a lot. There was no way during a lecture that I could listen, comprehend, and write down my notes with how quickly the professors spoke, especially during my first year. It was a very difficult task, although, with practice it did get easier and I had to depend on them less and less as the years went on.

Having help with my studies also freed up my social life schedule, if only a little bit. Although I'd never received any dancing instruction myself, I took up teaching dance classes on Saturdays at Arthur Murrays, which was right across from the medical school. I'd seen pretty girls coming in and out, and I went to the manager to see if I could get a job with them. The only position they had didn't pay anything, but I was fine with that. I just did it to meet the girls.

Although the first and second semesters of medical school were especially tough, I did well in a few subjects without too much outside help. Because a lot of it was memory work, copying information from slides, I did very well in biochemistry, histology, and embryology. Anatomy was just a fluke, the most difficult class of my college career that just so happened to come early on. The funny thing is that after such an awful experience with the subject that I still would end up becoming a surgeon.

Chapter 8: On Your Account

As usual, when summer came around, I went back to Montgomery and found a job. After such a difficult year, I looked forward to taking a sort of break and working instead. I don't remember what the job I originally took was, but a few days into the summer, I heard of another, more interesting opportunity. Rumor had it that a large percentage of the people in Washington, DC, had positive serology, which means they either had active syphilis or had been exposed to it and carried dormant syphilis. Syphilis is a serious bacterial disease, and it's highly contagious. In the general population, the number of people with Syphilis is probably less than 1 in 200,000. If a high percentage of DC's population had syphilis, it could very easily spread to be a contagion.

So the Public Health Services did everything they could to contain it. If the numbers were right, it seems like it might have been a necessary move, but there's no way that they would be allowed today to do what they did then. It's not politically correct for the government to make health decisions for you, even if it has a good chance of affecting the people around you. But back then, they got away with it. They collected people's blood and sent it to a lab to get checked. What I heard from other students in the program is that if your serology report came back as positive, the doctor sent you a telegram, informing you that you needed to report to a clinic for treatment. If you didn't report to the clinic yourself, the police picked you up and took you to the clinic, where you would get a spinal tap, to check to see if you had central nervous system problems, and you would be treated with Penicillin.

There was a lot of work to be done and Public Health Services couldn't get enough practicing doctors to cover it all. To make up for the deficit, they were hiring medical school students to go door to door to take people's blood. (The blood test they did was to test the blood sugar, which really was worthless, knowing what we know now.) They were offering $225 a month, which back then was good money. So I took advantage of the situation, applied and got accepted for the job, and moved right back to the ghetto in DC for the summer.

Going door to door in DC, you never knew who was going to answer. Sometimes I would accidentally interrupt activities at a drug house, and I would have to run very fast to get the hell out of there. Other times I found myself in places with lots of women, not necessarily prostitution houses, but as close as you can get. Most people there were happy to get the blood analysis done. But for most of the normal people I ran into, it was hard at first to convince them to let a random stranger into their home to take their blood. But after a few tries I realized that if I was confident enough and flashed my equipment, it was enough to earn their trust for the few minutes it took to take a vial of blood.

I helped at the clinic every now and then as well. I had no idea how to do a spinal tap, but the doctors there showed me and the other medical students once or twice and then let us do it ourselves. I was scared to death to do it, but it was more fun than going door to door and it paid a lot better, too. However, other medical students figured out that the clinic job was better and I couldn't always take a shift there. I spent most of the summer going door to door. One day, while doing just that, I met a woman who would make my life significantly more interesting.

At one particular house, a good-looking white girl answered the door. That caught me off guard a little, as she was one of the only white folks I'd yet to run across. But she was also having a hard time standing, which troubled me a little. Unshaken, though, I said with my vigorous approach, "I'm with the Public Health Services and I'm here to do a free blood analysis."

She was both sad and angry when she answered, "I don't want to see a doctor from anywhere for any reason. They messed me up. I can't walk."

I instantly felt sympathy for her. "Could you tell me what they did?"

"I had high blood pressure," she explained. "And they did some operation so that now anytime I stand up I almost faint."

They must have done some surgery for hypertension. It's a no-good operation that messes with nerves. It hurts more than it helps—it really just doesn't work.

"Now look," I told her. She seemed nice and at this point I really just wanted to help. "You don't have to give me a blood test. But I do think you should go see a doctor." I referred her to Dr. Evans. He was a tall, handsome, and imposing personality (at least to a student). He was also a professor of cardiology. "Go see him. I think he'll do the right thing for you."

She saw him and he earned her trust. They discovered that she had a Coarctation, which is a narrowing of an aorta. In other words, the heart has a huge blood vessel that sends blood to your arms and your brain. When you have a Coarctation, the artery gets very tight below the heart and very little blood goes through. This resulted in huge blood pressure elevation in her arms but none in her legs. They operated on her a while later and miraculously it worked. It's not a simple operation for adults. They usually perform it on children; the older you get the more dangerous of a procedure it can be.

Of course, I didn't know all this was happening at the time. At first, she was just some lady I had met while I was out gathering blood samples. But after her surgery, this lady made a really big effort to show me her gratitude. She looked me up, bought me cufflinks, and gave me a great, big hug to say thanks. I could also expect a Christmas card from her for years to come.

And then one day, a few months after meeting her, I got a call from a TV station in New York saying that they wanted me to appear on a program called On Your Account. It was produced by Procter & Gamble Productions, and it aired on CBS and NBC. The host's name was Dennis James. I asked what it was about and realized that it all came back to that same lady. It was one of those shows where it's supposed to look like they are reuniting two people who really had an effect on each other after years of being apart. But, of course, it would all really be prearranged.

It was scheduled to be filmed in the middle of the semester, and I'd have to take more than a day off to fly to New York. At first, I had reservations. "Look," I explained to the station when they invited me out. "I have an exam two or three days after this gig, and I'd like to prepare for it. I'm not sure I'll be able to make it." They told me they would pay for the flight and put me in the Waldorf Astoria. I told them I'd think about it.

I told John and Leonard about the phone call. They were more excited for the opportunity than I was. John said to me, "The Waldorf Astoria? Only kings stay there! You can't turn that down." When I protested with the same excuse about missing class, he added, "We'll take notes for you, don't worry."

So I went. It was a good decision, too, because I had the best meal of my life at the Waldorf Astoria. I was treated very well by the station. Not only did they put me in the hotel, they also gave me a medical bag full of instruments. I still have the bag, but I sold the instruments because I didn't need them at the time. At the school, they provided those things to the students. I should have kept them, but in the moment it was nice to have the money from selling them.

I appeared on a single episode of On Your Account. The nice lady who I'd helped came in first, and then I came in and she gave me a great big hug. I met Dennis James and we chatted for a bit. It really wasn't too bad of a time.

When it was all over a gorgeous girl came on set from backstage and said to me, "Your name is Farha." She used the Arabic rendition, which caught my attention. I complimented her pronunciation and waited expectantly to see what she'd say next. She asked if I had a sister by the name of Nazik. To this I asked, surprised, "My sister Nazik is very old. Her children are as old as I am. How did you know we were siblings?" It turned out that she was Lebanese, too. Her name was Janet Raheb. She recognized my name as Lebanese as well, she realized that she had some friends who knew Nazik.

Janet and I hit it off and started going out. She visited Washington from New York frequently. It seemed to be getting pretty serious. The only set back was that in Lebanese culture you don't get married until you are able to support your woman and your family. As a student, I still sometimes had a hard time getting a good dinner. Even after I finished medical school, I wouldn't be ready to support a family. I'd have to start my career and earn some money first. So, I dated her for two or three years, but once I moved out West, it was over.

My mother didn't like her, anyway. She met her and, being a mom, she began to interrogate her, one of the questions asking what her father did for a living. Janet told her he was a butcher—he owned his own shop in Brooklyn. In Lebanon, that's not a respectable profession. When I was growing up there, we could only get meat once a week, on Sundays. Most butchers in Judida were Muslims and they had no problems with butchering on Sunday. You have to remember that my mother and father were older and still lived in Lebanon, so they looked down on her for that. Afterwards, in private, Mother asked me if I was associating with the daughter of a butcher. I told her it was just fling, even though I really liked her. I knew that our relationship wasn't going to go anywhere because it would take me too long to get the money to support us. But Janet did keep in touch with me for some years to come after I graduated. I don't know what happened to her since, but I was glad to have met her; she was a very nice girl and very beautiful.

* * *

When the time came for my second year of medical school to begin, I didn't have to search for new roommates. Sam and John offered to have me live with them again, and since I liked living with them, I didn't hesitate to accept. Larry, on the other hand, found other roommates. For some reason, Larry wasn't very fond of Sam and John. But Sam and John were very fond of each other, and I was very fond of Sam and John's cooking. They included me in a lot of their meals, although I often objected to the expenses. I was happy to buy and consume cheaper, but less healthy, food and subsist on fewer than three glasses of milk a day. I really tried my best to save money for my parents as best I could.

At the beginning of the semester, Sam, John, and I moved into a one-bathroom, one-bedroom apartment with a living room in a nicer part of town. I took up residence in the living room, and Sam and John shared the bedroom.

I wasn't very observant. I was so uptight with medical school, my studies took over all of my time and my thoughts. I mean, I did do other things sometimes. For instance, I took time to date some girls, but it was usually a nurse who got off of work at 11 at night. So, like the previous year, I didn't spend a lot of time at home and I didn't notice the signs. I was oblivious. I didn't know how fond of each other Sam and John really were. They had their beds pushed together, but I had thought the reason for that was to give them more room. I would occasionally see them rub each other's back or perform other friendly acts, but I didn't think much of it.

And then one day, I had the facts pointed out to me. John Deré took me aside and said, "I want to talk to you." It sounded very serious, so I agreed to talk to him right at that moment. He insisted that we take a walk while we talked. I followed his lead, wondering what he could possibly want to talk about.

School was downtown, but there was a little park in front of the school, and that's where we headed to have a little privacy. I asked him what was going on. "Look," he said, "Everybody thinks you are homosexual."

So it was serious.

"You know I'm not," I said, a bit surprised. "We've been together with girls. You know me."

"I know," he answered. "But you live with John and Sam, and they are really... very close."

And that was when I first realized who I'd been living in the same apartment with for the past year. They were very much closeted. Looking back I could see that they had done little things while I was around, but they must have hardly ever exhibited those behaviors in public. John had a closer view of their relationship than most because he and Leonard were my best friends. They spent enough time with me at my apartment that they became close to Sam and John as well. But for people outside of our social circle to notice, Sam and John must have exhibited small behaviors that clued them in.

"Well, so what?" I asked, not understanding the big deal. "They're nice to me."

John considered this for a moment. He, Leonard, and I were all very accepting. I don't care what they do across the street as long as they don't force it down my throat. The problem was that I wasn't across the street. People were attributing John and Sam's behaviors to me.

"But everybody thinks you are a homosexual," he pressed again. "I think you ought to move out." I told him I'd think about it.

It just so happened that around that time there was an opening at Children's Hospital. If I took X-rays twice a week, they would give me a room in which to stay. It was a great opportunity and I took it quickly. But I moved out of my apartment with John and Sam only partly out of an interest in the internship position. You have to remember that this was around 1952, and homosexuality was still very much taboo. I personally didn't have anything against homosexuals, especially not ones who were my friends, but I also didn't want to be labeled erroneously. Although I moved out, John, Sam, and I remained good friends.

I never told them why I moved out; I just let them think it was for the internship. But of course, they never told me that they were gay, either.

* * *

George Washington is a great school, but, man, it was expensive, probably around $30,000 a year. It is even more now. Like any private (or even public) school, the tuition goes up every year. I felt sorry for my parents, because by the time George and I got our education, my parents had nearly no money left, and all of their real estate was gone by the time we graduated. I knew exactly what they had and it was very little. (But don't worry, we took care of them once our careers lifted off.)

Taking the position at the Children's Hospital offset my expenses a little, but I still needed to find a way to make extra money. Collecting blood samples was a great gig for the summer, but it wasn't sustainable during the semester since most of my time would be devoted to my studies. I wanted to find a way to make it work, though, as I was making good money and it was nice being able to do something medically related to earn a bit of cash on the side instead of working odd jobs. I went to the director of the project for the Public Health Services to see if I could get him to make a deal.

"You are hiring us to go door to door," I explained, "but the average collection is only about twenty vials per day." Most of the patients didn't want to allow you inside. These weren't the best neighborhoods, and they didn't like opening the door to strangers. "With those low numbers, it's costing you about seventy-five cents per head to hire collectors. Let me do it on my time, and I'll charge you only twenty-five cents a head."

He seemed to think it was a fine idea, but he expressed concern that I wouldn't make any money that way. He offered to pay me thirty or thirty-five cents a head instead. I thought that was a bonanza. I knew that I could go to the bus station and nab about ten people in fifteen minutes. And it was only a matter of time before I would find new gold mines.

I quickly discovered that I could make a lot of money at churches. I attended a few "Holy Roller" congregations to get to know a few preachers. It was a little bit of work but it was a lot of fun. When they get to rolling and singing and clapping, I enjoy it. Anyway, I'd take the preacher to dinner (on credit—not a credit card, but personal credit—the owner was Lebanese and we knew each other), and then the next day I'd visit him at his church wearing the white overcoat and stethoscope and every doctor instrument I could visibly wear to really sell the part. I'd tell him I was with the Public Health Services and we were doing blood analysis. Could I take the blood of the members of his congregation? Of course, he usually quickly agreed and on Sunday he'd let me set up in the basement of the church. During the services the preacher told his congregation that an official from the Public Health Services would be downstairs and that he wanted them all to go down and line up. I could get one hundred people, easy, on the weekends. That was $30 or $35 in one day!

At that point, I was making enough money and had enough traffic that I needed a little bit of help. There was paperwork that had to be done along with taking the blood—you needed to take the name and a phone number of each of the patients. I managed to get a couple of assistants, two student nurses, to help out. They'd take the information while I took the blood. And then one of the two would put a bandage where I'd inserted the needle.

Because I was doing so well for myself, I decided to let George in on the deal. I asked him what he was doing during the semester for money. He told me he worked in Tulane's library once in a while. He didn't make much. If he was able to get an entire week's worth of work done with his schedule, he would get $40. I told him I got paid that much in one afternoon and explained my deal with the director. I then suggested that he work with me for the Public Health Services come summer. He agreed.

When summer came, I was all set up. I had a place to stay, thanks to Garfield Hospital, which no longer exists. They had me doing histories and physicals in exchange for lodging. (I had no idea how to do either of those things, but they showed us, the interns, the basics and let us loose. All they needed was something to put on the patient's charts, so they didn't care much how well we did them.) I also purchased a card table to use as a booth and went to the local grocery store to ask if I could use a section of one of the refrigerators in the refrigeration aisle for a few of my things. I was afraid to say the word blood because I was afraid they would object. The manager agreed but told me to make sure to label what was mine. I never did end up telling them what I put inside.

I got ahold of George and asked if he was still willing to work in DC for the summer. He told me he had no money, so I sent him a bus ticket. Neither of us could afford to put George in his own room, so we shared the bed in my room at Garfield. It wasn't the most comfortable situation—we lived on the fourth floor and there was no elevator or air conditioning, not to mention we both snored significantly—but they didn't even know that he was there.

George and I spent the summer much the same way I spent my previous summer, only this time we weren't going door to door finding patients. We set ourselves up in big groups of people and did our work there, still being paid the per head amount that I'd negotiated with the director. George had a much different approach to the job than I did; he was not very aggressive. He didn't want to go out and get the patients like I did. I think it intimidated him trying to convince people that he was from the Public Health Department and that it was important that he take a sample of their blood for them. He had no problem working with patients who came to him, though. He would stick anyone that came to his chair of their own free will, and he was personable and efficient. He just wasn't proactive.

Nothing of considerable interest happened when we went back to school for our third year of studying medicine around 1956, except that I bought my first car. I wouldn't normally have spent the money on something so expensive, but I felt that it was necessary. I was required to travel to more than one hospital in the area, and there weren't street cars that went all the way out to some of the hospitals I needed to get to.

The owner of the Lebanese restaurant where I took the preachers knew someone who was selling a car. It was a 1947 or 1948 Plymouth, so it was almost a decade old. Who knew how many miles were on it. But the seller was asking for $450. Did I want to buy it?

I told him I couldn't afford it all at once, so he set up a plan for me to pay the car off in increments—$20 a month. It was a lousy car, but thankfully it lasted a long time. It took care of us, and we affectionately called it Nellie. It took me forever to pay her off, though. Not only did I have to make the monthly payments but I was also sinking a lot of money into her to fix her up. I didn't pay it off until the following summer, after George and I made a considerable amount of money through the Public Health Services.

That summer, we were featured in a photograph on the front page of the Washington Post. It was headlined "Medical Students Hungry for Blood," and our names were even in the paper. They basically gave us free advertising! I don't have a copy of it. I'm sure I could find it somewhere if I tried, but I never did. I was a medical student, I didn't care about being in the papers. I was stuck in survival mode. The only reason we found out was because Uncle William Farha told us. Somehow, that article ended up in Wichita, Kansas. When he saw it, he was curious because he didn't know any Farhas in Washington, DC. He investigated and learned that it was us. I'm glad he did, too, because he turned out to be a great contact to the Lebanese community in Kansas.

Partially thanks to the news and mostly thanks to our diligence, that last summer before graduation, we did really well with the blood sample collections. A little too well, in fact. I was working as a part-time employee, and there was a rule that part-time employees couldn't make more than $1,000 a month. The first month, I made more than the limit, so my boss gave me the thousand for that month, rolled the rest over into the next month, and told me not to make so much again. After that I always hit the limit but didn't go over. I had never been so rich in my life.

* * *

My final year of medical school was difficult for much different reasons than the first three years were. I was on call at one of the larger general hospitals in the area. They kept us on call for seventy-two hours, which meant that you didn't get any sleep for three days straight. Then you were allowed twelve hours to yourself to sleep, shave, and shower. After those twelve hours, you were expected right back at work again.

But that wasn't the only reason it was so difficult. I'd worked in other hospitals during my third year, and I could handle it. The difference was that for my senior year, I was placed on "dirty OB." It was the branch of obstetrics where you deal with patients who don't have access to reproductive healthcare and attempt to perform abortions themselves in "back alleys" with coat hangers. Those young girls came in very, very sick. The students in my class were the nurses and doctors who cared for them in this big general hospital, and we saw a lot of disgusting, horrible stuff. A lot of those girls died. The only drugs we could use were penicillin, an antibiotic, and sulfonamide, an antimicrobial. They were used in appropriate doses, but sometimes they weren't enough to reverse the damage that had been done.

Obstetrics can be a beautiful field. You can witness the miracle of birth over and over, and it really can bring a lot of happiness to both the doctor and the patient. But that year, I developed a tremendous disdain for obstetrics. Too many patients died under our care. We saw too much. I never wanted to work in obstetrics again, and I never did.

* * *

There are few times when I allow myself to get really, truly drunk. A warm night in July 1957, if I remember correctly, the night before my graduation from medical school, was one of those times. People were buying you drinks left and right, and you couldn't really refuse. It was the nature of the celebration, and I felt that I had earned it anyway. And so I drank drink after drink, until it started getting late. By the time I left the festivities, I was sloshed. I probably should have found someplace to crash nearby, but Janet was waiting up for me at a hotel we'd reserved for the night. So, against better judgment, I drove on the highways of Washington, DC, in an old car, inebriated, and by hook or crook I made it to the hotel where she had checked in. It really is a miracle that I didn't die, or kill anyone else, on the way there. I slept on the floor that night.

I wasn't used to drinking so much booze, so I slept in much later than I should have the next morning. My parents had come in from New Orleans (George's ceremony at Tulane was a couple of days before mine) and expected to meet up with me at my room in the hospital. I didn't think they'd get into Washington so quickly. I met up with them a little while later. They were a little upset that they hadn't been able to find me, but soon everyone was caught up in the excitement of graduation day.

Especially my father; he'd probably never been prouder of me than on that day. And he dressed up for the occasion. I don't know if you've seen a Shriner before, but it's a red stand-up hat that Turks wear, and it really stands out, especially in a room filled with Americans. It has a little tassel and everything. In Lebanon, we call those hats tarboushes. Well, to show his pride, my father wore a tarboush to my graduation. I tried to convince him to buy a new hat, but he wouldn't budge; he wanted to keep it. I was a little embarrassed, but it didn't seem like that big of a deal. The ceremony went off fine, but when they called my name, my father stood up, threw his hat in the air, and shouted with joy. He made quite a scene of it. That was when I got really embarrassed, mostly because it was a noticeably foreign thing to do.

Before my parents left to head back to Lebanon, I gave my father a thousand dollars to pay for his and my mother's tickets. I was still very conscious of their sacrifice, and I did whatever I could to alleviate the burden. But it was a mistake. He didn't need it at the time, and I didn't realize that I was only going to be making about $70 a month as a new intern.

Chapter 9: Internship and Residency

In those days, a year-long internship after medical school was required before you could complete your residency. I was determined to be in a university atmosphere, thinking that it would be the best education. It prepared you to go into academic medicine doing research or to go into teaching or to begin your own private practice. I'd only considered teaching in passing and I didn't particularly like research, but I wanted to keep my options open in case I changed my mind later on. Beginning the few days after graduation, George and I began our search for internships. We had no idea where we would end up, but we loaded up Nellie with two small suitcases full of what little clothing and belongings we had and drove.

Our first stop was Wichita, Kansas. Uncle William had invited us to some sort of Eastern Orthodox gathering there, and we figured it wouldn't hurt to visit. We'd keep our eyes out for internships while we were there. The thing is, we ended up staying in Kansas.

There were a lot of Lebanese people in Wichita, especially a lot of Farhas, and the Farhas were special people. They had an important part in the Wichita economy, because they ran their own supermarkets. In fact, they created some of the first large supermarkets in the West. They were rather innovative by nature. There were seven children in the family, who were brought to America by a widow. They sold newspapers and hustled until they could make work for themselves. Once they got their feet under them, they prospered. I was really impressed with the things they were able to accomplish.

There was also a huge hospital, the second largest in the

country at the time—St. Francis. George wanted to intern there and told me I should join him. Filling an internship at a private hospital was excellent training, but I refused, telling him I was going to intern with the University of Kansas (KU), which was in Lawrence, a couple hundred miles away. It had the atmosphere I wanted, so once again, George and I split ways.

Fortunately, one of the perks of the internship at KU was that you could eliminate any specialty you wanted. Due to my experiences my last year of medical school, I immediately ruled out obstetrics as an option.

Unfortunately, interning at a university was low budget. You had a semi-private room, which you shared with another intern, and the program did your laundry for you. But you were making only about $70 a month. You had to eat out of that, as well as put gas in the car and entertain the ladies. Money was tight for me; you would be surprised how many nights I went to bed hungry on that budget. George was making much more money in Wichita than I was.

Despite my little income, I also put money toward a $15,000 insurance policy payable to my parents in case something happened to me. It wasn't much, it amounted to only half a year's tuition, but it was all I could afford. I didn't want all of my parents' money going to waste. And my parents had been very kind to me with their money. All we had to do was write home and they'd send us however much we needed. I couldn't completely pay back their kindness, but at least it would be something. George thought the insurance policy was crazy. He and I were very much alike, but we were also very different.

Fortunately I found out from my friends in West Virginia that there were Farhas in Kansas City, and they put me in touch with the family of Sam Farha. Sam's family graciously helped to support me during my internship. I showed up for visits after I was off of work, which just so happened to be around dinnertime—just in the nick of time for some much needed food. I always told them I was just "in the neighborhood." But I think they knew right away that I needed some help. I lost of a lot of weight during my internship—not having a lot of money and not having a lot of time to eat anyway can do that to you. It got to the point that if I didn't show up, they'd call me! I must have eaten hundreds of meals there. It was a second home to me. I can even still remember their address.

There were many other Lebanese people there, too. I got along very well with them, and they always invited me over when I had the time. I usually went home from their social functions with an extra plate of food I could take to my room. They were wonderfully kind. Each family was composed of immigrants with a distinct air of success who started out in this country with nothing. Among them were the Swidens, who owned big stores, and the Eddys (an Americanized name), who became a prominent family when they developed grain elevators and banks and very famous restaurants in Kansas City. The Eddys also became influential in politics—whoever they supported for governor in Oklahoma City usually got the job. I was lucky to have friends like these, so willing to help another Lebanese immigrant make something of himself.

I had a lot of good times as an intern. I worked hard but I also played hard. There were a lot of nurses, mostly women, there. Most of the guys in the program were married—they weren't foreigners like me. I was single, still stuck in the notion that I wouldn't start a family until I could support them. For the others, things were less traditional. Their wives worked or they took out student loans. But that was fine, because that meant that there were a lot of available women for me!

Dating during my internship was less than glamorous, unfortunately. I didn't drive my car, because half the time I couldn't afford to keep enough gas in the tank to go anywhere. If I wanted to take a girl out, there were few options. If the girl had a car we could go out. But if she wanted something to eat, she'd have to pay for both of us. It was a simple as that. If she did not have a car, we'd go back to her apartment and we'd cook or something. If the girl was really lucky and I had money at the first of the month, I would take her out to pizza. There was a pizza place walking distance from the KU medical center. You could get a pizza and pitcher of beer for a few dollars.

Girls didn't take up all of my time. A lot of the staff, interns and paramedical alike, threw parties. It helped me to get to know a few of my coworkers in a little more intimate of a way. I was particularly impressed by a surgeon named Fred Kittle, who we called "Red Fred," because of his bright red hair. I don't know whether or not he's still alive. He was married, but he never missed a party, even if he had to come alone. He was a handsome young man, and the girls liked him quite a bit, which led eventually to his divorce. But he was very good surgeon.

Of course, it doesn't take much to impress an intern because he doesn't know very much! Whether or not he deserved it, Fred impressed me, so I was complimented when he told me I should stay at KU for my residency after my internship was over. The professor of surgery also wanted me to stay at KU, but he had different opinions about my future. He wanted me to go do research in the laboratory. As much as I liked Red Fred, I didn't want to risk being stuck in a lab for my entire residency. So I applied and got accepted to the University of Virginia at Charlottesville, which had a very nice academic atmosphere. But I did decide to become a general surgeon, just like Fred.

Thus, at or near the end of 1957, I began my residency. Being at the University of Virginia really made me realize that I was still a foreigner. I hadn't fully assimilated yet. I felt a little excluded, although I wouldn't say that people were necessarily prejudiced against me. I traveled a little bit in the South and saw prejudice first hand, and my treatment was nowhere near as bad. There, I definitely saw blacks and whites being treated differently, although I didn't comprehend it at the time. I hadn't learned much of American history at that point. For interactions with me, I just sensed that people used a different approach. They could hear my big accent and noticed that I was a little unusual, so they were a little standoffish.

I liked the University of Virginia enough to stay there for two years of my residency. The pay wasn't any better as a resident than it was as an intern, about $70 a month. But at the University of Virginia, you didn't have to pay for food, and you got a private room. They also provided us with uniforms, which most of us lived in. It was nice not having to pay for new clothes. Most of us didn't even have a coat, even though it got cold at times. The girls were also very pretty and I made friends with a bunch of them. Despite these perks, I didn't really foster any attachments to the program.

When my third year residency was coming closer, I realized that they were going to stick me in the laboratory just like they had thought of doing at KU. I did not want to spend a single year researching in the lab. I was too anxious to take care of patients. The closer I got to practicing medicine on my own, the more I thought of my time following my brother-in-law around in Lebanon. It was fascinating the respect he got from his patients and the things he was able to accomplish in the wilderness, where he had nothing compared to what we have now. Imagine the things I could accomplish with my education!

You don't normally approach the chief of the program to ask for assistance in transferring to another program, but I didn't know that. I was not very sophisticated. So I innocently went to my professor Dr. Mueller for help. He was a distinguished surgeon, very well-known and very busy, and yet he made time to see me.

"Sir," I said when I met with him. "I need some help. I am afraid I would not be good for your laboratory. I'm just not made for that. I want to get into clinical medicine. I would like for you to help me get into another place." In other words I was quitting.

It was a poor time to come to him. Positions were about to change. But I couldn't help that I wasn't aware of the changes that were about to be made. I didn't know I was going into the lab until the last month of my second year of residency in general surgery.

He looked at me, smiled, and was very gentle and understanding. "Jim, you're a little late. But I'll do all I can. Where do you want to go?"

I told him I wanted to go to California, to any university there. I'd never been there before and I wanted the experience.

Moving there didn't seem like a big deal to me. I had a car, and I could find my way across the country with a few cheap sandwiches. Things were different then. It was safe to pull over and sleep in a rest stop.

He said he'd try and to come back in two days. So I did. When I saw him the second time, he told me that he couldn't find me a spot at a university in California but that he'd found a spot in a private hospital, if I wanted that. I didn't. He had an alternative, though. Another third-year resident who was attending the University of Utah had just been drafted, leaving a vacancy in their program. I was a perfect fit for the job, but if I wanted it, I had to be there by a specific date. It would be a bit of a crunch, but I was sure I could make it.

I thanked him. "Do you know anything about Utah?" he asked.

"No," I answered honestly.

"Do you know anything about Salt Lake?"

"No," I said again. "I've never even heard of it. But if you say it's a good university, that's good enough for me."

Nazmiah Farha (sister), Jamil Farha (father) and niece

Family and friends in the old country.
Dr. George second from right in back row; Dr. Jim waving, front row

Friends of Dr. George, in the old country. Dr. George is fourth from left.

Dr. Jim's 1957 visit to Lebanon.
Jamil Farha (father) far left third row; Dr. Jim holding niece,
third row; Wadia Farha (mother) far right third row.

Alex Ammar (nephew) baptism
Front row: (L to R) Dr. George Farha, Violette Ammar, Alex's grandmother;
Back row: Dr. Jim Farha; and members of the Ammar family

(L to R) Philip Farha, friend, Wadia Farha (brother-in-law), Dr. George Farha,
friend, Fayez, friend in Lebanon

Gathering of elite Muslims and Christians.
Front, wearing Tarbouch, Jamil Farha (father)

Entire family of Wadia & Jamil Farha
Back row: Fayez, Jim, Georgette, Violette, Suad, George
Front row: Nazik, Wadia, Jamil, Nazmiah

Photo taken in Kfeir, mother's birthplace.
Back row: Fayez, Georgette, friend, friend, Wadia, Suhayl, Violette, Fuad,
Mikhael and wife. Front row: Ghassan, George, Leila Mikhael

Jim (right) with friends from boarding school - Alay.

Early family photo
Back row: Wadia (mother) Nazmiah, Nazik, Jamil (father), Fayez
Front row: Suad, Georgette (seated)

Fayez and Violette

Political demonstration in Lebanon – Jim is in back left corner

Dr. Jim and Dr. George with their mother

Fayez with friends

Chapter 10: Darla

You would hardly suspect that residents work in hospitals as apprentice-level doctors with the pay they take home and the lifestyles they lead. When I packed all of my belongings into Nellie to make my way across the country to the vast desert of Utah, it probably looked more like I was visiting than it looked like I was picking up my life and moving across the country. I had maybe a single suitcase with clothing and a few textbooks.

Before heading west, I drove to West Virginia to see the Shdeeds and the Farhas who had been so kind to George and me during our undergrad years. It was nice to see them again, and I knew that I was going to miss them a lot while I was away. They had always been so kind and generous to me, making me feel like family. Saleem Farha especially was a kind and gentle man. He taught me a lot as a new adult, and I looked up to him a lot. I was also as comfortable with him as if he were my own father. And I knew that I wasn't going to make it to Utah without some money for gas.

"Uncle Sam," I asked when I had a minute alone with him. "I need to borrow some money. I'm going to Salt Lake City to continue my education."

"How much do you need?" He asked.

"Around $200," I answered. I could tell from the look on his face that it was probably a little bit more than he had expected. "I promise I'll pay you back, but I'm not sure how long it will take." I had no idea what kind of money I'd be making at the University of Utah, and honestly I didn't really care as long as I could make do. Money was irrelevant; I just wanted to get the education.

He only had to take a second to think it over. "All right, but I'm going to make you pay it, no matter what."

I spent a single night in West Virginia and then drove nonstop—aside from stopping on the side of the road to sleep—to Utah. The trip was a long one, and despite my roadside naps, I was exhausted. There are a lot of beautiful mountains and valleys surrounding that area in the southwest, but after so many hours, I don't think I'd ever been happier to see buildings once again.

When I arrived in the city, I got out of the car and started asking around for directions to the county hospital, which was run by the university. It was an odd phenomenon. After asking a few, very different, people where it was, I kept getting the same answer: "We don't have a county hospital."

I was insanely exhausted and beginning to get a little frustrated. It's difficult to maintain good manners when you are running on no sleep. I was finally fed up and asked someone, "Isn't this Salt Lake City?"

"No," was the much more polite reply. "You're in Ogden."

And so I got back in the car to drive from the place that I thought was Salt Lake City to the actual place that was Salt Lake City, another forty-five minute drive. Once I was in the right spot, it didn't take me long to find the county hospital. The first and only thing I did when I got in was find the intern's quarters—which is where the interns sleep when they are on call—and crash. I wasn't worried about anyone stealing my meager belongings, so I just left them in the car.

I registered with the program the next morning. It didn't get past them that I'd used the intern's quarters when I was decidedly not an intern, but they weren't upset. They kindly told me that I could stay there for a few days, but I would have to find a place as soon as possible.

When I discovered what my salary would be, I decided to stay in the intern quarters until they booted me out. I would only be making somewhere around $125 a month as a third year resident. On that, I had to pay the rent, eat, put gas in the car, and entertain the ladies. I could stay in the intern quarters for free, and I got away with it for two months. Eventually, though, they wouldn't tolerate it any longer and they came to me and said, "Now look, Doctor. You can't stay here. You have to find a place."

And so I found a place. It was near the hospital, and I was lucky to be paying very little. There was an old lady who had two rooms in her house she was renting out. It was fine at first, but then she started asking nosy questions. She always wanted to know when I'd be coming in or leaving, and she was always peeking when she thought I wasn't looking, or even often when it was obvious I was. It wasn't long before I got tired of that and decided I needed to find an apartment for myself.

I rented an apartment in a not-so-good neighborhood. Utah's not-so-good neighborhoods aren't nearly as bad as DC's are, so it definitely was not the worst I've lived in. But it also definitely was not the best apartment I lived in either. It was a one-bedroom apartment without any locks, and half the windows were broken besides. I think I paid $21 for rent and utilities, all inclusive. The heat was supplied by a little gas heater in the middle of the room. It was very slim living in terms of living arrangements. Luckily I was provided with some food. I used to wait in the evening to get a sandwich or two from the area where they had food for the guys on call. There was always plenty of extra sandwiches, so I managed to bring a little bit home sometimes.

It was at this time in my life that I found my wife. I met her the first day I walked in to work as assistant chief resident. I walked into somebody's office and there was this gorgeous young woman, one of the prettiest I'd ever seen. Surprised at seeing someone like her in the office, I asked her what she was doing there. She informed me that she was helping my professor with his genetics research. She was a student from a nearby college, Brigham Young University (BYU). But she was just working there for the summer before going back to school. I asked her name. It was Darla.

I was hooked from our first conversation. Darla was one of the most personable people I'd ever met. She was sweet and kind, and it didn't take me long to realize that everyone who ever met Darla instantly liked her. It certainly didn't take me long to like her.

I found out that she liked dancing—Spanish dancing, with the Castanet, in particular. Apparently, she was very good at it, too. At age 12, she even taught dancing from her garage. Suddenly I was glad for my amateur days at the Arthur Murray's dance hall. I imposed myself on her, trying to impress her. I offered to take her home that night in my Rolls Royce. (That was quite the bluff. Nellie often had to be pushed just to get started. I made sure to always park on top of a hill, just in case.) I think that intimidated her. Combined with the fact that I was at least eight years her elder, it probably had quite the effect on her image of me. I was probably the only single person in the entire house staff at the hospital. But whether she was intimidated or impressed, skeptical or amused, she agreed. It was the beginning of a beautiful, hard-won relationship.

* * *

Before moving to Salt Lake City, I'd never even heard of the Mormon Church.

Here's a little story to show you how ignorant I was. The chief resident of my program's name was Larry Stevens. He was the kindest guy, and I really liked working with him. But there was something really strange about him that I couldn't quite explain. Every time he changed clothes while we were in the same room, I got a glimpse of his undergarments, which looked oddly homemade. After days of wondering and keeping silent, I finally admitted to him, "I'm interested in your underwear. It's kind of strange. Is it something your mom or your wife makes?" He took the abrupt question rather well, explaining that they were something he wore after he was married in the temple. He also told me that he was a "bishop" in his ward, which I discovered had quite a different meaning in the Mormon Church than it has in most Christian denominations. Well that got me interested in learning more about the Mormon Church, and I looked into it. I even read the

Book of Mormon. It interested me enough to learn a bit, but I quickly discovered that the church wasn't for me.

It was good to learn more about the culture and religion of many of the people who were living around me at that time, though. In those days, most everyone in Salt Lake City and the surrounding area was a Mormon (now it's only about half, mostly because California is diluting them—I would say unfortunately). I hadn't even realized that so many of my neighbors had a common religion! I also quickly made the connection that students at BYU were all Mormon. Little did I realize the obstacle that would put in my and Darla's relationship.

I was about as far from Mormon that you could get. I smoked, I drank, I gambled, and I used four-letter words. It was distressing to her family when we started going out. Not only were they a churchgoing family, but they were of a pioneer background. They expected great things from each of their children, and that included each of them marrying within the faith in a Mormon temple. Darla wouldn't be able to do that with me.

Unless I converted. That was the first attempt for the family to come to terms with my dating their daughter. I respected them, so I agreed with their demands. They tried very hard. I met with many Mormon authorities. They invited me to church on Sunday and to other activities during the week. They did everything they could to try to spark my interest in the church. But no matter what they tried, I didn't feel that it was a church I wanted to join. I noticed the Mormons kids I worked with were outstanding kids. I knew they raised very good families. But tradition is difficult to overcome. I always thought I was an Orthodox—I was born an Orthodox and I will die as one. And just like Darla couldn't get herself to convert to Orthodox Christianity later in our courtship, I couldn't get myself to convert to Mormonism.

Darla didn't seem to mind as much as the rest of her family that I didn't want to convert to the church. I liked her family and I was kind to them, and that seemed good enough for her.

We worked hard to make our relationship work despite any sort of discomfort that came from our peers. And we had a good time.

It's tough to find someone as wonderful as Darla. I knew I was lucky the moment we started dating. She was beautiful. She was smart. She was congenial. And, perhaps most attractive, she really was a great dancer. As a result, many of our dates took place at a club on State Street. There was a cover charge of $2, which back then was meaningful, even if it doesn't seem like much money now. We couldn't afford much else after that, so I would order her the shrimp cocktail and I got myself a beer. That was it—those sustained us the entire evening. But the food and drinks weren't the reason we went there anyway. It was the dancing that caught our fancy.

They had an open floor, and Darla took to it like a fish to water. I wasn't bad myself, and together we made a great team. In fact, we danced so well, and so often, that the manager dropped our cover charges and gave us beer on the house. (They couldn't give us the shrimp cocktail free, though.) It was a great deal, so that was our go-to spot when we were dating.

She also tried her best to make my apartment a comfortable living space. She didn't seem to mind that I had no money, but she did what she could to lighten my home up. Home renovation and decoration would become a passion of hers over the years, and it was in my little, ghetto apartment in Salt Lake City that I first saw glimpses of this. The place really was a disaster. My bed was falling apart, and so I had it resting on my trunk for support. And I didn't clean the place up very well. With all the smoking and drinking I did, it was usually pretty filthy. But Darla covered the walls with burlap and did the best she could to lighten things up. We called it the Tent of Omar Khayyam, after the Arabic philosopher who coined the term "Drink and be merry for tomorrow you may die." She made a tent and her brother made us a little couch. Those were great improvements, considering.

We dated for a long time. We became inseparable. When Darla didn't get home by 11:30 at night, the phone in my apartment would ring, because her family knew right where she was. Whenever I wasn't working, I was with Darla.

When after a few months of dating our relationship started to get more serious and I still hadn't converted, Darla's family tried a new angle. Just as hard as they tried to bring me into their church, they tried to convince Darla to leave the country to proselytize for the church. But Darla didn't want to go on a mission. So she came up with a plan of her own.

"Let's get engaged." She said.

"Okay, we're engaged," I said only half-joking.

"It's not that easy," she informed me. "You have to buy a ring, and we have to throw an engagement party. This is serious."

"What's the big rush?" I asked. At this point, I was still "old country." There was no way I was going to get married until I had a sustainable income. I was only twenty-nine years old; I was too young to get married!

But I knew she was getting a lot of pressure from her family to break things off with me. I was a big risk to them, and I can't really blame them. I'm not the kind of person that I would want my own daughters to date, and it was even worse coming from a Mormon point of view. But I liked Darla a lot, and I didn't want to lose her. So when this talk of engagement became a regular plea, I began to fear that if I didn't ask her to marry me, she was going to quit me. It was either I give in to the pressure from her or she give in to the pressure from her family. I gave in first.

I gathered $30 as quickly as I could and gave it to her to buy herself a ring. A little while later we invited a few people over to the apartment for an engagement party, complete with some potato chips, Coke, and beer. We were officially engaged.

I thought that we were home free after that, but I was wrong. A couple of months into our engagement, Darla informed me that she was still getting pressure from her family to leave me, to get out of town and never look back. She thought we should get married. We'd been engaged for long enough after all.

The problem was that I was still a resident and I had zero money. Not only could I not afford to provide for a wife and children, I couldn't even afford to host a wedding in the first place! But it didn't matter to her. She put a lot of pressure on me and, once again, not wanting to lose her I gave in. I found the money easily enough.

I had met a few Lebanese people in Salt Lake City who I quickly became friends with. One was a young (although older than me) lawyer, the mayor of Bountiful. His name was George Fadel. He was magnificent to Darla and me. He and our other friend, George Haddad, took good care of us. George Haddad owned a big and tall shop. Those two Georges bought us dinners and often took us in to their homes. They were successful, and they were generous with their time and money. They both owned horses, and Fadel owned practically half of Bountiful then. We developed long-lasting relationships with them. I still call them two or three times a year.

George Haddad is 94 and he's still very sharp on the phone. He bought a huge mountain back in the day for practically nothing, but everyone told him he was crazy for doing it. It turned out to be a huge investment. I think that George Fadel is still alive, too, but whenever I call I can't seem to catch him.

Anyway, I used to play poker with them and a few practicing physicians in the area. We always did it at my place. They weren't allowed to play poker at home; they had to do it in secret because they were good churchgoing people. We all bet heavy, with a buy-in of maybe $20.

One night I won $800. That's what I used to pay for my wedding.

The wedding wasn't an overly extravagant affair. We invited only Darla's family, George, and a few residents from the hospital, and our honeymoon lasted for only two days. But we made sure to follow as many of the old country traditions as we could. I bought (rather than rented) my own tuxedo as well as wedding party gifts. George travelled all the way from Boston to be my best man. He brought a stack of one-dollar bills with him.

Darla's family wasn't happy that she was going to be married outside the temple, but they supported us how they could as well. And even Darla and I had religious differences in a significant way. We ended up getting married in a non-denominational church, but I wanted Darla to become a member of the Eastern Orthodox Church. In Lebanon it's tradition for the woman to join the man's church. Period. That's automatic. And that's what I thought she should do. But she had a little difficulty.

There was a Greek Orthodox Church in Salt Lake City, but unfortunately the priest there was not very good. All he did was bash the Mormon Church, and that's not exactly the best way to gain influence. She took lessons as valiantly as she could, but she came to me after about a month and told me that she couldn't do it. She didn't like the priest, his presentation was simply horrible, and if we wanted this to work, we'd have to find a different way to do it. I told her it was okay if she didn't join the church after all but that all of our children would be Orthodox.

It wasn't that I was super invested in Orthodox Christianity; it was just the way I was raised. It was tradition, and tradition to me was something that was important to uphold. I'm not even that good of a Christian. I'm a Christian with my own theology, who does not always conform to the Church. I don't think that my church is the only church; it's a big part of the reason I couldn't become a Mormon. I don't voice strong contradictory opinions, but I don't personally believe in a lot of the things that Christian churches preach. I am content being a Christian, though, and I believe the church instills good values into our communities.

Throughout our marriage, my in-laws continued to attempt very hard to get me converted to Mormonism. I never converted, but Darla continued to participate actively in the Mormon Church throughout our marriage. That became a particular issue of contention while we raised our children in Wichita. It was an obstacle we had to deal with every step of the way. Darla and I had a good life, but it wasn't always smooth sailing. It never is for anyone. But we had both decided and insisted that marriages have to go forever—divorce was not in our vocabulary. I think it was mostly due to Darla's efforts and her genius behavior that we survived. Our marriage worked because of her and her demeanor and her strong foundation and good basic Christian principles. For instance, we never went to bed angry—that was Darla's rule. Whatever argument we had during the day, it had to be settled before bed. And Darla and I had a truly happy marriage.

Although my initial attraction to Darla was physical, it didn't take me long to discover that she was just as beautiful on the inside as she was on the outside. There might be wives out there in the world who are as good as Darla was, but let me assure you that they are very difficult to find. She really was one in a million. During our marriage, we survived on very little. I was chief resident when we married, and I still had a few years to go before I would start making a real, sustainable salary. But we made it work, and Darla never complained. She even worked while we lived in Utah, to help us keep up with our expenses. She had to forget about continuing her education because she had to stay home and take care of our first baby, Maria, but she made a little bit of an income on the side as a typist.

If there was anything that consistently upset Darla in our marriage, though, it was my forgetfulness about dates. Due to my background and culture, I don't have a mind for anniversaries of any kind—birthdays, holidays, or (perhaps most important to Darla) wedding anniversaries. I wasn't prepared for, because I didn't remember, our first year anniversary. But boy oh boy, did I remember our anniversary after that first year. And her birthdays. I forgot the kids' birthdays a few times, but my wife always took care of them. As an American, my wife was very much used to celebrating holidays and birthdays.

I think I made it up to her, though. Once we could afford it, we replaced her thirty-dollar ring with one that had a big diamond. My daughter has it now. It was one of our prized possessions, because I was able to get such a great deal on it. I was always a dealmaker, having learned early on that if I wanted to keep any of the money I earned I had to be careful with it. Eventually Darla had more jewelry than she needed. I liked to buy gold for her; I knew it would always have value, despite the fluctuating market and I didn't feel that it was frivolous or a waste. It got to the point that she finally told me that she didn't want any more gold!

I don't think that either of us had any regrets about the way that we lived, both when we were poor and once we had more than enough money. Darla had a passion for life and the people around her. She loved everybody, everyone loved her, and she took an active part in the community. She volunteered in children's homes, and she fought for principles she believed in. When we had the money for it, she even put her money where her mouth was. As an outspoken activist, she rallied for anti-abortion and anti-war causes and eventually it gained a lot of momentum. She also donated a lot to the art museum. When I was making money, she pulled me into a lot of things I was grateful for.

Chapter 11: Training in Utah

I finished my training in Utah after completing my fifth year's residency. As a fifth year resident, you become chief resident. When you are a chief resident, you run the program, or at least that's how things were run in Utah. As the chief resident, I had to okay each surgery that required the operating room being used in off hours. Of course, that only applied to cases inside the program, not anything that was instigated by a professor.

As a chief resident I rotated through the Veteran's Administration Hospital. If you hear that there's corruption in that hospital, I can affirm that it's true. It's worse than anything you read or heard, and it's been corrupt for decades. I personally think the VA hospital should be closed and vets should get government assistance to get private care. How do I know all this?

I almost got fired at the VA because I was so efficient.

I maintained 120 percent occupancy because of their foolish system. Let's say you had a hernia operation and after a week in the hospital, they send you home and tell you to come back to the clinic in two weeks for a check-up. They maintain you in the hospital system as an in-patient for the entire three weeks, even though you are at home for two of them. It was a rather inefficient system that made it difficult for people to get the care that they desperately needed.

I'd call to take in a patient because he needed surgery, and I'd be refused because according to the system they didn't have any beds. But when I'd go to check the actual floor of the hospital, I discovered that half of the beds were empty. Each time it happened, I picked an empty bed for my patient, which meant the bed was singly occupied but double-booked. Having technically over 100 percent occupancy was bad for administrators and budgets and all those other things they care about, so I got called to my boss's office. He was very upset and he told me I couldn't do it anymore. It was against the law. I was on thin ice and I had to be careful.

I didn't care at first. I was helping people, and that was much more important to me than any negative consequences I might incur. So I kept doing it. He called me in again and said that if I did it again he'd have no choice but to fire me. I had to back off, but it angered me. The beds were empty but they were full. "Filling" them made for bonuses in the budget, and it was the only reason they ran the hospital that way. Of course I'm speaking from memory and actual numbers may not be accurate.

I was glad when my rotation was over and I went back to the county hospital, where I finished my residency around 1963. I'd mainly focused on general surgery and thoracic surgery. I was considering the prospect of becoming a cardiothoracic surgeon, but I wasn't really sure if I liked it or not. There wasn't much of that sort of surgery being done at the University of Utah, so I didn't get good training for it there.

The next step was passing my boards, so I took the exams for both general surgery and thoracic surgery. Where you went to pass your boards was regional, and one of the spots available for Utah doctors was in Los Angeles. I can't remember if there was a closer spot I could have gone to, but LA is where we ended up. I'd been wanting to experience California for years, but this was the first time I had the chance. Darla made the drive out there with me. We had had to get rid of "Nellie" a little while before, and we were still broke at the time, so we borrowed my father-in-law's car for the trip. We stayed in a motel that was in a somewhat dangerous neighborhood near some university or other, and the next morning I started my exams.

It was very intimidating to have a bunch of older doctors

judging your medical knowledge. There were lots of technical questions. What is the basic chemical composition of plaque? How many esophageal cancers are there? And all the while they were throwing slides at you, asking you questions about things that you haven't seen before. I held my own, though, and I passed both boards.

While we were in the area, I got a job offer to work as a general surgeon, doing some thoracic surgery. Darla and I found a private place to live, too, at a great deal. As part of the deal with the hospital, I would get a place to live, a car, and $35,000 a year. It would be millionaire's living.

When George found out that I was planning on moving out to LA, he was floored. "Why the heck do you want to go to LA? We've worked on getting to this point together, so let's stick together now, too. Besides, Wichita is a really great opportunity—there's nothing here. You could start heart surgery here if you really wanted. You can do a lot of things." He explained to me that there were a few general surgeons, but most surgeries were being done by family doctors. Can you imagine that? Non-surgeons performing not just a few surgeries but most of them! It was a recipe for disaster.

George convinced me. The opportunity was there, and it was one I didn't want to pass up. The problem was that there was a law in Kansas that you couldn't practice medicine unless you were a citizen, and I wasn't a citizen yet. But I did have my green card.

Knowing that I would eventually be making a career of surgery somewhere in America, I started the paperwork to become a citizen during my residency—you had to get started early because you had to hold a green card for five years before you could apply for citizenship. I was a little late, though, so I applied for my green card as "urgently needed." My professor wrote a letter to that effect, which was approved, thanks to some of my connections to Senator Chappelle through one of my uncles. I never actually met him, but one of his aides took me through various offices in Washington to get the paperwork through. All that was left was to leave the country and come back with the card.

I was going to go to Canada because it was close and it seemed more convenient. When George found out, he was dumbfounded. He asked me why I didn't just go home for a week or two. I had mixed feelings about going home. It had been about nine years since I'd been, and I didn't know how different it would be, or how different I would be toward it. I didn't have the money to travel so far, anyway. Realizing these were excuses, George asked me how much I needed. I asked for a thousand, which he couldn't afford either as he was still a resident at the time, too. So he ended up borrowing a thousand dollars from someone—he had people in Wichita who would cosign with him on anything. They loved him there.

So I went back to Lebanon. It was strange to be back, but definitely not as bad as I initially thought it might be. It was around 1959, and things had improved a little but not a whole lot. I couldn't say much about the country, anyway, since my shoes and clothes weren't very good. When my father saw the state of me, he was embarrassed, so he went and bought me new clothes and shoes, which was generous of him. It was nice to be able to spend a little bit of time with my parents, who had gotten me to the point that I was at.

I got back to America with only $25 to my name, but I had a green card, and that's what counted. All I had to do was wait for five years and I would become a citizen of the country that I had grown to love so much.

When George invited me to come and practice with him in Wichita, I still had six months to kill before I could take the citizenship test, swear in, and officially became a citizen of the United States. (It used to be quite the process back in the day.)

I talked to George about my plans and he suggested that I stay in Utah and watch some heart surgery. Since I wasn't sure which direction I wanted to take—general surgery or cardiothoracic surgery—it could help me to make up my mind before taking the big steps in Wichita. And the LDS Hospital was making great strides in heart surgery at the time. Why not see if I could get a spot on the staff there?

I had to admit it was a good idea. When Darla and I got back to Salt Lake City, I talked to my boss and asked if there was a place for me at the LDS Hospital. They had two very prominent surgeons at the time—Russ Nelson, who was one of the finest surgeons I've ever seen, and Ray Rumel, who was so innovative that he made many of his instruments in his garage. Both went down in heart surgery history as pioneers in the field. They were also part of a big group of cardiothoracic surgeons and were doing a lot of heart surgery. They were doing very innovative procedures—valve replacement, congenital heart surgery, all sorts of things that were yet to be established into the basic heart surgery repertoire. The mid-1960s was the middle ages of heart surgery, but they were leading them to the enlightenment. The hospital was getting referrals from the entire intermountain area, all the way to California.

My boss got me a contract to work there for six months. I loved it more than I could have imagined, being in the midst of such advances in the field. I decided right away that I preferred cardiothoracic surgery to general surgery, and I asked my boss if he could get the hospital to extend the contract for another six months. He had to jump through a few hoops—they had to put me on the payroll, since I was making two or three hundred dollars a month—but he managed to do it. I am most grateful to Dr. Walter Burdette, the Professor of Surgery, and the one who allowed me to continue on the payroll and arranged the LDS Hospital venture, which was great. Dr. Burdette had recommended me for citizenship in earlier years.

Around the end of my first six-month contract, I got my citizenship. Darla helped me study for the exam. Then we scheduled a day for the swearing in and headed down to the courthouse. It was a remarkable day. The judge asked a few questions, I took the oath, and I was officially a citizen of the greatest country on earth, the United States of America. This was in about 1964.

I was mostly assimilated at that time, although you don't fully Americanize for ten to fifteen years. Even now, decades later, there are things about the culture I don't know. I don't know all of the Christmas carols in English. I've never been able to read the funnies like some people and actually think it's funny. My kids make fun of me sometimes because there are gaps in my American cultural knowledge and finesse. There are just some things you never really master.

Chapter 12: Practicing Medicine in Wichita

Wichita was in a bad way when George and I first got our practices started. A very high number of the surgeries being performed in the city were being done by family doctors, which meant that the quality of surgery was not the best. While I was taking calls on the weekends, I saw some truly unpleasant things. One time, during my first or second year, George called me up and asked me to finish a gall bladder and common duct exploration. I knew something must have been wrong, since he nearly never asked me to finish procedures for him. I asked him what was the matter. He told me that he had to go and do an ileal bladder. He sounded rushed and a bit frustrated. I couldn't understand why—it's a big procedure, but it's almost never an emergency. I asked him again what was the matter. What was going on?

"Don't argue with me, please. Come up now. I gotta go." And he hung up.

Not at all miffed, but a bit curious, I hung up, changed clothes, went in, and finished the case. There were no complications on my end. George had a much more eventful time that day than I did. I got the details from George later.

This lady went in to see a family doctor. She had a mass in her lower abdomen, and she wanted to have it checked out. The doctor consulted with her and determined that she had an ovarian cyst. That's a pretty serious condition, so he recommended she have it removed as soon as possible. He took her to the operating room, opened her up, and he took it out. It seemed a simple enough operation for him at the time. However, when the nurse was putting some dressing on the area, she noticed some blood in the vagina, which seemed out of place. The blood was coming through the urethra.

The nurse was concerned, so she informed the doctor. He was sure nothing was wrong, but just to be sure, he told the nurse to phone a urologist to come and check it out for him. When the urologist arrived, he made an interesting discovery. He put the scope in the urethra and all he saw was bowels. There was no bladder.

The doctor had removed her urinary bladder!

Once it's out, you can't just put it back in. In fact, it's up in the pathology lab now. But that was a mistake I never heard of before or since. Every good surgeon knows that the first thing you do with a woman who has a lower abdominal mass is insert a Foley catheter to make sure it's not an obstructed bladder. But the doctor didn't even recognize the organ as a bladder. He didn't have the training for it. He took it out, thinking it was a cyst, and he closed the patient up.

Not believing that he could have made such a mistake, the doctor called George to come and take a look at the specimen he took out. George confirmed it; it was the bladder. So they had to open the poor woman up again so they could reconstruct the intestine and hook the ureters so that the urine could exit safely. You hook three or four pieces of bowel to create a new conduit from which the urine can exit the body safely.

She was only forty years old. Other than having her bowels completely rearranged for problems beyond her control, she was a healthy woman. She should have sued him for malpractice. Luckily for him, she came to the ICU about forty days after the operation with an acute myocardial infarction and died. So she never had the chance.

The doctor received only minimal punishment, equivalent to a slap on the wrist. George and I thought that they should have prevented him from doing any surgeries from then on. Period. But we were new in town, and stirring up the water would have only hurt our businesses and reputations. Specialists like us depended on referrals from family doctors. If we had alienated the family doctors, we wouldn't see another case again. So we had to let it go. At least that time, and maybe a time or two after that. Fixing the system was gradual.

I was personally involved in another interesting case that was much less dramatic. Wichita had so few surgeons that family doctors were doing hysterectomies and bowel resection. They were allowed to perform on a gall bladder, but they couldn't do anything to the common duct. Well, the two are connected and sometimes the gall bladder stone can go in there. It is extremely irresponsible to give someone privileges to do a colon resection when he can't do a common duct. I think if you are going to open the belly, you should be able to deal with almost anything in there.

Well, one morning when I was working at one of the hospitals, I got called to the operating room. "The doctor needs you right away," they said. I rushed to help him and found him in a bit of a situation.

"There was a little lump in here," he explained quickly, "and I was trying to fix it and sh** came out." Those were his exact words.

"You must be in the colon if fecal matter is coming out." I said, half amused and half concerned.

"Yeah, I think so too." He said. It was pretty obvious that that was the case, but I guess he wanted a professional opinion. We worked together to fix up the poor woman. She had to have a colostomy and wait a long time and clean the bowel and hook it back together. Luckily she didn't become septic.

This doctor was not quite as inexperienced as the one who had removed a woman's bladder. He learned from the experience and quickly recognized that the woman had had a hernia, called a Richter's hernia. That's what happens when some people have a defect in the belly wall, and a piece of colon gets caught in there. It makes it feel as though it's just a little lump, maybe a tumor or cyst that needs to be removed. So that's what he thought needed to be done. He learned though. I don't think he ever made that mistake a second time. Cases were documented where a doctor had removed half the gallbladder and bragged about doing it in 10 – 15 minutes. Except the patient came back with an acute GB.

It was because of these kinds of mistakes that George realized there was a great opportunity for specialists like himself (and me) to set up new practices in Wichita. When he invited me out to Wichita to set up my practice alongside his, I didn't even consider staying in Salt Lake City. It was already full of surgeons, and I would have been fighting with dozens of people for business. (It was worse than other places where people were making strides in the medical field; in Utah, you had people from all over the country flocking to Utah to start a practice there. All of the Mormons wanted to end up back in Zion.) If you want to have any business, you have to go were the openings were, and there were definitely openings in Wichita.

It wasn't much of a sacrifice moving to Wichita, though. George had already developed quite the following there, friendly and professional relationships alike. He was established as a medical authority there, someone who was not only friendly but could also be trusted to do a good job. He'd spend his entire residency at St. Francis Hospital in Wichita, leaving only to fulfill a fellowship at the Lahey Clinic in Boston, which was a very prestigious institution. It was the clinic for pancreatic duodenal surgery, and it was worth his spending a bit of time away from the place he was in love with. George truly was the best General Surgeon I have ever seen!

The opportunity to be close to George again, and this time fulfilling our father's dream for us as doctors, was an exciting prospect. But if I knew then just how difficult it was going to be starting up my own practice, I wouldn't have done it. The long hours, the politics, the physical and mental exertion—if I had to do it over again, I don't know if I would have felt that it was worth it. I might have tried to start my practice somewhere a bit easier, where surgery was already standing on its own.

Our difficulties started as soon as we set foot out of Utah. Darla, Maria (our first daughter), and I started our trip to Wichita easily enough. We climbed into the Volkswagen, putting a rack on top of the car to hold our trunk and suitcase. Unfortunately, we didn't get very far that way. Because of the resistance, the car wouldn't go 40 miles per hour downhill, even if you floored it. Realizing it would take days to get to Wichita with all of our belongings, we decided to stop at Rock Spring, Wyoming, and ship the clothes to Wichita from there instead of bringing them along.

Thinking our problems were behind us, we set out again. After a few hours of driving, though, we had to stop for a second time. Our baby girl, Maria, got sick and there was no way we could continue the trip in her condition. We stayed the night at a hotel, which not only cost us an extra day of travel but also took an additional forty or fifty bucks from our meager savings. By the time we got to Wichita, I think I had eighteen bucks left to my name. What I wouldn't have given to have a thousand dollars sewn into my pants.

We were broke. Not Clinton in the White House broke, but really, truly broke. For the first few months I even worked performing pre-employment physicals for $5.50 a head. I had advanced training as a cardiac surgeon, and I was performing physicals for cash! I was nobody yet. I had to make a name for myself before I could really get any traction in the town. Once Darla and I settled a bit, I went to every ER and told them that anytime they needed a doctor for any reason, I was available. (In those days there were no ER physicians. You went to the ER, they asked who your doctor was, and they'd call him. Then he decided if he would come in and see you or if he'd just let the intern on call see you.)

Because we hadn't had a chance to visit Wichita to find accommodations, and because we couldn't afford anything at the time anyway, we stayed in George's basement for a time. George had been in Wichita practicing there for a year at that point, and he was already beginning to gain some traction in town. He'd made lots of friends with the family doctors, and so when he returned from Boston, the referrals were pouring in. He was already doing very well for himself.

Even though it wasn't a place of our own, living in George's basement was more comfortable than we could have asked for, despite a few hitches here and there. For the first few days, Darla had no clothes because they were still on the train from Rock Spring. She purchased a few items from the Salvation Army or some thrift shop to get her by in the meantime. She was such a great lady that inconveniences like that didn't rattle her. She was steady as she goes and very pleasant, always happy, with a big smile.

When the clothes finally did come, George took one look at my wardrobe and told me I needed to go and buy a whole new set. I told him I didn't have any money, and he told me I didn't need any—I just had to sign my name. So, on credit, I bought a suit, a hat, and a few shirts and ties. I was excited for the new wardrobe, but I was just as anxious to pay my debt off. I didn't like to borrow money. We worked for a few months and when Christmas came we did some money distribution and bonuses. I looked forward to the relief of paying off my debt. But when I went to the shop to pay it, they informed me that I didn't owe anything. I was confused, thinking maybe I'd gone to the wrong place. But no, I'd bought my clothes there. What had happened? I had a sneaking suspicion.

I called George, told him what had happened, and asked if he had anything to do with it. He told me he had taken care of it. He knew I didn't have any money, so he paid my bills, all of them. He was providing a home and utilities to my family and he made sure that our other necessities were taken care of. And when we moved out of his house and into our own place, he even gave us the couch from his basement. There was no way I could express enough gratitude for all of the things that he did for me and my small family. But we were the best of friends and I think he could tell how grateful I was. Incidentally, I "never" repaid George the previous $1,000 or the cost of the clothes!

Having George was a help to me on the business end as well. He was very supportive at every stage. He'd already established his own office, and he allowed me to join him there. He even changed the name for me when I came into town.

One of the many reasons that George loved Wichita was that the presence of so many Farhas already in the community meant that he didn't have to spell his name out for people that often. But when I came in, there were two Dr. Farhas, and that got confusing quickly. When people addressed "Dr. Farha," both George and I answered. So we decided to go by our first names instead. But I soon decided that "Suhayl" was too difficult to remember; I wanted it to be easy for doctors to remember my name and refer their patients to me. And so people started calling me Dr. Jim.

It took a while to get used to how things ran in Wichita. I thought it was odd that so many of the surgeries were being done by doctors who didn't have surgical training. We'd tried convincing the surgical sections of the medical board to pass rules that made it so only certified practitioners could perform surgeries, but those were quickly voted down. There weren't enough surgeons to get that sort of momentum going. And when surgeons voted for those sorts of changes, family doctors felt that they were trying to keep them from doing business. The physicians would stop sending referrals to the surgeons, which was the only thing that kept their own businesses going. So there wasn't much personal benefit in voting for change.

I got sick of it really fast. I couldn't understand how George had managed to practice in Wichita so long under such conditions. I voiced my concerns with him, telling him how ridiculous I thought the situation was and how we were at a dead end. But George had more hope than me. "Let's give it time," he said. And then he worked some magic.

George was very personable and he'd already begun to develop small relationships with the physicians in town. Once he got to know a few primary physicians, he started putting ideas in their heads. "You are very important, you know," he'd tell them. "You physicians fill your own niche that no one else can, and we surgeons depend on you. You shouldn't have to be grouped with the surgical section—you should have your own group! You're specialists—you have a family practice specialty. We should start respecting that, and you should be able to form your own section and run your business your way." That made them feel good. They went off on their own and stopped voting in the surgical section. The problem was solved, thanks to George.

From then on the surgeons had the freedom to make our own rules. The first order of business was to limit the practitioners who have surgical privileges in the hospitals in Wichita to those who were board certified. The surgical board was no rubber stamp—it was a very difficult board to pass. There's probably between a twenty to thirty percent failure rate, and if I recall correctly it can only be taken three times. After that, you are out of luck.

Changing the requirements that way established a standard of excellence in surgery, which really benefitted the hospitals. St. Francis, the largest hospital in town, took to the changes first, and Wesley was not far behind. I would have to say that George takes most of the credit on that one, with David Street being a very important contributor. We all helped, but they engineered it softly and gentlemanly. They kept everyone happy.

Before the surgical section was made up exclusively of surgeons, many of the surgeries left Wichita to go somewhere else, usually to the Mayo Clinic. There just wasn't enough room for growth to attract surgeons to the area when everything was being controlled by family physicians. It was a very different era, surgically. But George and I worked very hard to change that. Once we'd gained control of surgeries in the hospital, we did everything we could to keep the patients in town. The first step was to keep qualified surgeons in charge of surgery at the hospital, but the next step was to make sure that private surgeons had a network to support them.

And so George and I started our own surgical group. It started out small, and George and I really made all of the decisions. The group didn't really grow large enough to have a board of directors until a few years in. Like the medical boards at the hospitals, we made a rule that to be able to join the group, you had to be board certified or board eligible.

There was one exception. There's no need to mention his name, so we'll just call him John. John was a good surgeon, well trained—as you would expect since he was one of our trainees. He trained under George's supervision, but I knew him very well. He was a great guy and he was very smart. For some reason, though, he just couldn't pass his boards. He froze up every time. When on his final attempt he didn't make it, we decided to overrule our own rules and he stayed in the group. We also made sure he had privileges with the hospitals, as we were in a position to influence the decisions of the certain sections.

George and I were the only owners of the group for a while, but soon we realized that we needed a third. George found the man for the job in one of the residents under his tutelage: David Street.

David was a nice American boy, very gentle and very well-liked. He trained with us as a resident, specializing in general surgery, and he was a superior trainee. George was the director in the program for general surgery in St. Francis, so he spent a significant amount of time with David and saw his skills and personality firsthand. They had a very special relationship. I think George talked to him and managed to convince him that he should go to the Lahey Clinic to spend a year just like George had.

I had just come on the scene when George was training David, but I was very impressed by him, too. He was a special person. When he was to return from Boston, George asked me what I thought of getting him to join us as a partner in the group.

"I don't know," I replied. I liked him a lot, but the group was still in its infancy. "I don't even have much to do yet. What do you think he would do?"

"We'll figure something out," George said. "He's a great guy and I think we could use him."

George turned out to be right, as usual. David really was an excellent surgeon, very smooth and highly respected. He also had a lot of integrity and pride. During the Vietnam War, for instance, we were told (perhaps erroneously) that we could show legitimate reason to avoid the draft. David wouldn't have that. "If I'm drafted," he said. "I have to go." And he was drafted, but he did not have to go overseas. He was assigned to a U.S. hospital in the military system. (A few members of the group were drafted as surgeons, actually, and some had more than one tour of duty, the younger ones participating in the Iraq War as well.)

So we asked David to be a partner, at twenty percent instead of the forty percent share that George and I each held. We were only willing to split ownership because we thought he would complement the group whether we needed him surgically or not. He added our initial thrust into forming the group, and my worries were proven unnecessary. He soon became quite busy. While George was spending time at St. Francis, David began to go to Wesley so they didn't compete with each other. I went to both (or all three once St. Joseph was built) because I was trying to stick to my specialty, cardiothoracic, as well as vascular surgery.

David became very close to George and me, almost like a younger brother. In fact, we even passed along George's now-famous couch from the basement. When Darla and I had first moved out from his basement, it was the only piece of furniture we owned. But little by little, as I became more established and made more income, I bought furniture from Salvation Army stores—couches, tables, even a few bunk beds by the time we had multiple kids—and we passed the couch on to David, to become the only piece of furniture that he owned until he got his feet under him.

And so the group Farha, Farha, and Street was born. That name didn't last long because we didn't like that it sounded like a law firm. So we changed it. I thought it should be the Farha Surgical Group, but it became the Wichita Surgical Group. George, always the considerate one, said we should just call it that so that no feelings get hurt; some people might not like being lumped into the Farha business. But the community still called it the Farha Surgical Group because we were so dominant in it for so long. Eventually it became the Wichita Surgical Specialists (WSS). When we were getting ready to exit, seven or eight years after we changed the name the first time, we wanted it to have a fresh name and to really relinquish it so that anybody who wanted could buy a share.

Once David was in place, we each had an important role to take on. As the chairman of the department of surgery George was growing the general surgery program. The medical students at the University of Kansas had the choice during the last two years of study to stay at KU or to come to Wichita. Wichita was always more in demand than KU because the students made rounds with the attending physician, who paid a lot more attention to them than they would get at the university. We were also finally gaining traction as a group, which helped the program to expand even more. He started with things like kidney transplants and went on until we finally embarked on cardiac transplants and other transplant programs.

David was very influential in the program as well because he was very good with the students and residents who came through. I didn't interact nearly as much with medical students and residents as David and George did. Especially not George. I was the chief of cardiothoracic surgery, but that was still a small program that I was working to enlarge. It was my job to develop the program and secure its various elements, a job that's a lot easier to say than to do. I gave a few lectures here and there, but I really was too busy to do much else, since I had to go between all three of the hospitals to work on cases. The work we did for the university didn't pay much of anything. Being chiefs of our departments really only meant holding clinical titles, not the traditional professorial tenure. In fact, most of us just returned the money we earned, if it was insignificant enough, back to the university budget.

I had my work cut out for me trying to establish heart surgery in such a medically conservative town. There was a vacuum not only in Wichita but in all of Kansas. The University of Kansas, for instance, was doing poorly. But when you really throw yourself into a project, you get hooked. The alternative suddenly disappears, and giving up is not an option. By the time we got going, we were doing many more surgeries than the University of Kansas was.

I also had a lot of work to do in developing the business side of running a practice. The minute I got to Wichita, I started promoting myself and George. There weren't very many options for promoting a medical practice. Back in the day, advertising was unethical and it was very much frowned upon, but we did a lot of marketing. The only way to advertise was to write articles (which I did), travel and give talks (which I did), and to make good relationships with family doctors who would send referrals your way when surgeries needed to be done (which George did). It killed two birds with one stone, giving talks. Because of my affiliation with the University, there were a certain number of post-graduate Continuing Medical Education hours I had to fill. So I gave a lot of talks.

Beginning my practice as a cardiac surgeon was difficult, but fortunately for me, there was a group of cardiologists who helped me to attain my goals—they were the main reason I succeeded in cardiac surgery.

Ernie Crow, who is dead now, was the senior member of the group. He was truly the most magnificent physician I ever encountered; he embodied everything positive you would ever want see in a physician. Then there was William (Bill) Hayes, who was a brilliant doctor. He was my boss when I was an intern at the University of Kansas, and he was very supportive of my career path. Finally there was Frank Brosius, who was only semi-supportive. He talked a good game but didn't live up to it.

Participating in their group helped me to establish my name in the community. Word got around that I was a good doctor, and that I knew what I was doing. However, none of the hospitals in Wichita (or really all of Kansas) had the resources to perform the kinds of surgeries I wanted to be doing. Ernie and the others would send me referrals, but they were small heart cases like patent ductus or Coarctation. These didn't require big surgeries. They didn't require open-heart surgery or pump (otherwise known as extra-corporeal circulation) surgery.

I decided to leave the group after only a few years because it was a difficult atmosphere to work in. There was a lot of unfriendly competition, and there was a lot of politics involved in decision making. It was part of the reason I didn't get any of the big procedures I wanted. Many of the surgeons didn't support my decision to do cardiac. They felt that if they couldn't do the kind of surgery I was looking for, it couldn't be done! It was a terrible thing. When I got going and started scheduling major surgeries, they were very interested to see if the patients lived or died.

When I told Ernie Crow that I was going to leave, he warned me that the going would be tough. There had been a lot of problems in the community with a doctor who preceded me. He was not a heart surgeon but pretended to be, and he inflicted a lot of harm on the community. It might have just been hearsay, but apparently there was even a "student nurse who died in his office after being drugged". It was going to take a lot of work to gain the trust of the people again. Ernie tried to convince me to stay with the group—they would take it slow and eventually they would get to the point where I wanted to be. I thanked him for his concern, but I had a bigger plan in mind.

I worked very hard to get cardiac surgeries going in Wichita. There was even an eight-year period during which I never took a single day of vacation. My hard work paid off. Around 1967, my staff and I began to do some real heart surgery. It wasn't pump surgery, but it was bigger than the Coarctation surgeries I had been doing a year before. It was called the Weinberg Procedure, devised by a doctor of the same name in Canada. Retrospectively, it was a poor procedure. It only worked if the patient survived six months, giving their arteries enough time to communicate. But I performed enough of them successfully to establish myself as a trustworthy doctor in the community.

From there we were able to convince the hospital that we

needed to have pump surgery. If we wanted more patients from Kansas to use Kansas hospitals, instead of outsourcing, we needed to have the equipment to perform the surgeries they needed in house. The hospital appropriated $2,300 for a pump and equipment, which was very little money. It wasn't enough to pay for any decent equipment, but it was the only money we had so we had to find a way to make it work for us.

I found out that a friend of mine, Nazih Zuhdi, was in Oklahoma City running a successful private practice. He had helped Dr. Walton Lillehei to develop a double helical system for open heart surgery. It was very inexpensive to put up—you could do it in the garage. It was not the most efficient pump surgery, but it worked. So I started taking regular trips to Oklahoma City. First I learned from his technician to set the pump for him and watched him perform a few surgeries. Then I took my technician to learn to set the pump. After we were sure we had the nuts and bolts of the thing down, we built the pump in someone's garage in Oklahoma City.

We started out small after that. We sent a few people to go and buy condemned dogs—who were going to be gassed—to practice on. It helped to train the nurses, and it also helped me to develop my own techniques. To keep up with advances in the field, I did a lot of travelling to watch other people do procedures that I'd never seen, or sometimes even heard of, before. (You have to keep in mind that in the 1960s heart surgery was in its infancy.) I sometimes went out of state to watch cases (for instance Houston), but I most often went to the Cleveland Clinic to watch cases. The first bypass surgery was done at the Cleveland Clinic, to the right coronary artery. I'd never seen bypasses done in my training, so the Cleveland Clinic is where I was first exposed to that sort of procedure. It helped that I participated in some cutting-edge surgeries at the LDS Hospital in Salt Lake City. I was never the leading surgeon during those procedures, but it's usually pretty simple to apply the basics of surgery to any specialty. You don't have to see every single procedure to be able to perform them yourself. Surgery is surgery. As long as you know the area you are working on, you have the basic ingredients to perform any kind of surgery. It helped that I saw so many different cardiothoracic procedures, but I also learned a lot on the job.

That first year, my practice had ten cases scheduled. The hospital only let us do one case a week because it tied up the blood bank, or at least so they claimed. They told us that it was all the operating room would tolerate. It was a struggle getting them to agree to even that. I was still a little player in the medical game at that point, so it didn't make much difference what I said. I had to keep going to Ernie Crow to pull strings for me. It was a good thing he wasn't upset over my leaving the group. But because of our combined efforts, we were able to perform each one of those ten cases, and we didn't lose a single one.

My practice didn't grow much until two years later, in 1969, when Ernie called with a case that would change the game in Wichita surgery forever. He told me he had a patient who needed an aortic valve replacement. That's a biggie.

"You think we're ready to do that?" I asked. I was nervous. I'd never done one, although I'd seen several.

"It's now or never," he said.

So I took the case head on. I remember the patient's name was Miller. I don't suppose I'll ever forget it. I was able to successfully perform the valve replacement and he had a full recovery. From there on, my practice just increased. We got more cases, and we got better at doing them.

Meanwhile, the Wichita Surgical Group grew by addition. After David Street joined, we had another doctor, Chuck Jenny from Emporia, join. After a while we were starting to get a lot of cases, especially for organ transplants. We started out with kidney transplants. There was a colonel in the military, Chuck Shield, who wanted to get out, and he was doing kidney transplants in the military. We got him and he did a great job getting that started in Wichita. After that worked out so well, George had the idea to do heart transplants as well. I didn't want to do heart transplants, because they always seemed to come in middle of the night, and if you have a big schedule the next day, it could become quite tiring. We had a young man who was excellent with his hands in the group. His name was Tom Estep, and he had been trained in heart transplant, but he hadn't done it in six or seven years. So we sent him, a magnificent surgeon, to various centers to where he would spend a couple of months to refresh his cardiac transplant training. He was originally trained in Indianapolis, where they already did heart transplants. But he needed a refresher course. He traveled and he was wonderful. He did 125 cardiac transplants without a single hospital death. But he was selective, and I thought that was very smart. He was a great surgeon.

Soon we were doing liver transplants, heart transplants, and other transplants along with all of our other surgeries. We couldn't do it all ourselves, and my brother managed to bring a lot of surgeons in. I helped only a little. Unfortunately, it was sometimes hard to find someone who fit a specific specialty. When we decided to bring that kidney transplant surgeon in, for example, we learned quickly that he had a forceful personality. But we could handle it, because he did a great job as a renal transplant surgeon. He was the head of the transplant in the Midwest.

I would say retrospectively and respectfully that a better selection was had amongst the general surgeons, because they were vetted for so long right under our noses. George was fortunate in his sections because he was able to snatch many of the surgeons from those who were in training under him, after knowing them well for four or five years. He knew exactly what kind of work they could do and what kind of issues they brought along. Because my specialty was so specific, I always had to go outside the program and rely on supportive documents for future associates. It was the normal process for me—interviews, looking at their training, and reading letters of recommendation. How much can you evaluate someone from pieces of paper? You can evaluate him on an institutional basis (see how well he did and from where), but you don't know that he can assimilate into the family of the group.

Eventually, though, we added eight cardiac surgeons to the

group. It was a great help because eventually we were doing more cases than the University of Kansas was, and it used to take two of us to do a single heart case. In those days we did not use any physician's assistants or nurse clinicians. Now things have changed—they only use one surgeon, and the physician's assistant helps with the case. I'm glad I didn't have to do it like that.

When we brought others in, they were employees, not partners. We owned everything in that operation, but nobody worked harder than we did, and very few kept up with us. George looked at every incomplete surgical case or legal case or delinquent payment. We seldom sent anyone to a collection agency, choosing instead to work with our patients to keep their loyalty. I looked at every cardiothoracic and chest case. It was our group, and we had responsibility over it.

George and I also alternated being on call at the local hospital, which really was for emergencies only. It was one of the largest in the nation (it had seven or eight hundred beds at one point, although it has since shrunk), and I think it benefitted from our help. As a result, I worked as a general surgeon on weekends only. I didn't like doing general surgery anymore, now that I'd begun to specialize in heart surgery. It had been a couple of years since I'd really done it.

Needless to say, after the first few years in Wichita I was very busy with all of my responsibilities. Add on top of that the fact that Darla and I were having more children, and you are beginning to see why beginning my own practice was such a difficult task.

George and I were both very driven. We both had a goal to be the best and the busiest surgeons in the state, maybe even the country. I'm not sure that I accomplished it, but I sure did try. We had to write off about 28 percent of all charges, meaning they didn't pay anything. But we were still making a lot of money, so we didn't mind that much. Our patients came first. When the phone rang, we always answered it; we never let the answering service pick it up. When a doctor called, he was accommodated. If he wanted a patient seen the next day, he'd be seen the next day.

In fact, nothing was postponed until the next day if I could help it. I might have been overworking myself a bit, but my compulsive nature wouldn't let me have it any other way. Even when I was busy, every consult was answered the same day. Sometimes I would be doing surgery all day and I had three or four consultations that I wasn't aware of until five or six in the evening, because my nurse would take the information (there was nothing I could do while I was in surgery). But I always made time to see those patients on the same day they came in, unless the physician specifically specified on the paperwork "Do not see until tomorrow." They'd learned that if they didn't say that, I'd be seeing the patient the same day, and sometimes that's not convenient for everybody.

I also took care of burn patients, which is something no one really wants to do. They are really messy, they take a long time, and they are truly heartbreaking. There's really no plus side to that except helping someone who has been through a great misfortune.

We also never charged a nurse or her family or a doctor or his family. Never. The same principle applied to preachers. If they had insurance, we'd collect on that, but if there was a balance, they never saw a bill. That sort of service isn't expected, or provided, in offices and clinics anymore. It's a little sad how traditions die out.

We had certain codes that we followed. For instance, I was a careful surgeon. I didn't leave a single thing to chance. I never got a lawsuit in thirty-five years, even though I did high-risk surgery. The average surgeon gets sued every five years. Some surgeons got so many lawsuits that they had to go under extenuating circumstances to continue practicing in Wichita. Someone supervised them for a year, and then they could continue their practice. Most of the time people were sued because they goofed up. Sometimes you can get sued for stupid things that you shouldn't have allowed to happen, for instance turning over a patient you operated on to a family doctor. You should always remain in control of the patient. You are the captain. When members of the group slipped up, they usually didn't do anything seriously wrong, they just needed a little bit of help. But that never happened to me because I had a way that I followed.

* * *

Although George, David, and I ran the group, when the group got big enough we created a board of directors who participated heavily in running the group.

We sometimes made decisions that weren't well liked, like doing heart transplants. It was expensive and it was dangerous, being pretty new in the field. But other decisions were liked well enough, like the slush fund. The group paid for certain things, like equipment, personnel, or travel (for people who need training or something like that), for projects that really accomplished purposes of the entire group. It was the easiest way to get the funding for the people who really needed it. This way we didn't have to go to everybody and say, "We're going to need this or that from you." Instead, we determined how things were managed and took the money straight out of the slush fund.

It also helped keep sensitivity in some of the more personal matters. There were a few people in the group who did not produce enough income for their livelihood but who were essential to the wellness of the group. For instance, take a new surgeon with a limited specialty. He's going to be operating on young children, most of whom have no coverage. But he's going to operate on them whether or not they have insurance, which makes his income suffer. That's bad for him and it's bad for the group. It's very important to have a complete group. You need a variety of surgical specialists and if you want them to keep doing what they are doing, you are going to have to subsidize them somehow. The slush fund was designed to help supplement their income without any embarrassment. If a certain specialist was needed to complete the group but the demand was small in the community, we still added him to the group so that we could be a full-service surgical group.

The slush fund also helped us when we started doing heart

transplants. It cost a lot of money. We wanted to be able to do our transplants first class, so we sent Tom Estep to Philadelphia and San Francisco to watch transplants at hospitals there. That got expensive quickly, since we not only had to pay for him to travel, but we had to get him an apartment, have him come home on weekends, and help pay for other miscellaneous expenses. There's no way I would have been able to fund that on my own. That also came out of the slush fund.

After a few years of practicing medicine, when our cardiothoracic section really started building up, I got a new partner. His name was Jim Newby, and he was one of the best partners I ever had. He was a well-trained surgeon who started out with the Wichita Clinic—our competition. But we were doing a lot of heart surgery and they were doing nothing. We invited him to join us, and he didn't hesitate to jump ship.

He was a great addition; he gave us the boost right when we needed it most. I was still using the double helical system, which was really inefficient. It took longer to do each case with it than it would have to use a different pump machine. We had to cool the patients' bodies because the heart-lung machine couldn't pump enough blood to them during surgery. He knew that the heart-lung machine wasn't very efficient but it was safe, but it took him a little while to speak up about it. He was a gentle person, and I think he was afraid of stepping on anyone's toes. There are a lot of different ways to come to your boss to tell them that something needs to be changed. If you pick the wrong time or tactic, there might be resistance.

Sooner or later he asked, though. During one of his cases, he asked, "Jim, do you mind if I use this new machine?"

"Sure, sure," I said, not really caring what kind of equipment we used as long as it got the job done. "You can use whatever you'd like."

Gosh, the machine he used was so great that bang! we discarded the old one immediately. And this time around we had a bit of money so we bought three pumps, one to put in each hospital, instead of making our own in someone's garage.

Our group subsidized those purchases, too. We hired nurses to run it that our group paid for. But it became economically unsustainable for us to keep doing that, because the insurance would not pay for the pump or for the nurses. So we gave the pumps to the hospitals and then turned it to be a hospital function. Now it's a big corporate thing; pump technicians even have unions.

* * *

I did a lot of firsts in Wichita. I did a lot of vascular cases, mostly because there was another surgeon doing vascular surgery in Wichita and he was having very bad results. But his failures saw my success. I did the first carotid artery surgery, cleaning it out. I did the first valve replacement in Wichita, which was a big one. I did the first bypasses in Wichita. I was lucky to have the opportunity to do so many things in Wichita and contribute to the field I'd dedicated my life to. Training programs in the 50's and 60's didn't expose you to everything new, things were always changing.

Once I'd won the struggle to get heart surgery started in Wichita, I was invited to send members of my team to other towns to start heart surgery there as well. I was not in favor of it. It didn't seem right to send a surgeon seventy miles away to a small town without the infrastructure to support an open heart procedure and to have him there alone or maybe send someone to help him occasionally. So we passed on it. Despite this, they are doing heart surgery in Salina, Kansas, and Hutchison, Kansas, and I don't know where else. I personally think it's a little risky. I'd rather have my (or my family's) heart surgery be done in a place where they do two or three or four heart cases a day, instead of two a month. I want it to be routine, not a big deal. There are so many little elements you depend on doing heart surgery. It's not just the surgeon. The surgeon is the most important element, but there's an infrastructure you have to depend on, and it just isn't there in small towns.

I also had some very unusual cases. For instance, I had a case after a mother's car rolled over an eleven-month-old baby.

To make a long story short, the little baby was almost dead, and I was the only guy available to do surgery. I did a tracheostomy (which is when you make an incision in the windpipe, or bronchus, to get air flow) on her and put in chest tubes. Later on we found out the whole bronchus to the right lung was cut or blocked. It healed closed, which made it so that no air could get in or out and that lung collapsed. It was a serious problem. If the lung was totally collapsed, the lung wouldn't get infected, because there's nothing going in and out. But if it was only partially collapsed, it would get destroyed and endanger the young girl's life.

I didn't know what to do. That tube is so tiny at 11 months old; I didn't know if I would be able to operate on it. I called a lot of people asking for help. Finally someone gave me sage advice: "Jim, why are you so worried? Try to repair it. If it works, great. If it doesn't, just take the lung out." That advice came from a prominent surgeon in Denver, whose name I cannot recall but I will always be grateful to him.

I calmed down after that. Luckily, the surgery went very well and we did end up repairing it. It was a miracle. I reviewed the literature that year (all the way up to 1965), and there was no other case using the same procedure that was successfully repaired on anyone under two years old because the bronchus is so small. I was lucky. And she was lucky.

I met her when she was 48, at my brother's funeral. I had followed her medically for eighteen years and then lost track of her, but I didn't make contact. So when George died, she knew that a Dr. Farha had saved her life, and she had thought he was the one who did it. She brought along her picture and the article from the newspaper that told about her accident framed together. When I informed her that I was the doctor who did the operation, she gave them to me as a gift. I still have it in my office at Wichita. She's still alive and well even now, and a grandmother. I will never forget that case.

And we did a lot of cases. Altogether, the group, from its inception to about 2012, totaled one million surgical procedures. It trained a couple hundred surgeons who went to many places in the U.S. and it also trained hundreds of medical students. It was one of the largest private surgical groups in the nation, if not the largest. Despite having such high numbers, each of us was always busy. There was a lot of surgery to do in Kansas, and our practice dominated the entire state. We were also getting out-of-state referrals, people from Northern Oklahoma, Missouri, all the way to the Colorado border.

Throughout the years, the group gained and maintained a superior reputation. If you are in the WSS, you are automatically perceived as being a good doctor, someone you can trust with your healthcare.

To me, this was the fulfillment of the American dream. If George and I can do it, many can duplicate it. This business of relying on handouts is destructive to people's souls and ambition. I know a lot of people feel held back by their backgrounds, but there's prejudice everywhere. It isn't so concentrated in America that it really holds you back. If you are willing to put in the work, you can achieve your dreams. Honestly, if George and I can make it in a very conservative, Bible belt, Wichita community (which is definitely not so international), the door should be open for many others to make it.

George and I have seen the fruits of our efforts. The group still exists, but George and I own nothing in it. It's now being run by my nephew, who has done a great job with it. It still has maybe forty surgeons involved in it, and it's the premier group in the Midwest. They've also kept up the tradition of having each member be board-certified. He himself has to take his boards every five years. It's a very controlled, and profitable, setup. I don't go and visit often. As a surgeon, you know, you see so many things that you don't like. But I've been there as a patient, to see one of the neurosurgeons. George was there as a patient, too. He had an abdominal aneurism and had one of the guys operate.

In the end, we decided that it really was the surgeons' group, not ours, even though we organized it. They deserved a share at an appropriate price. And we really weren't business-minded people, looking to turn a profit wherever we could. We didn't feel that as owners we should have received a premium for their hard work. The money we got from selling it didn't even come close to paying for our retirement. We just wanted anyone who wanted to buy a share to be able to afford it. They had done a lot to build it up; they could own it now.

We had also collected a great deal of memories in and affection for the group. We were the ones who started it and slaved over it. We had competed with over one hundred other doctors for the chance to operate on the residents in Kansas. The population of Wichita hasn't increased very much, but there was a considerably higher amount of surgery being done there because of the work we did as a group. We didn't want to sell it to some random entity or corporation who hadn't put their blood, sweat, and tears into it just as much as we had. So we sold it for a small price to the surgeon who deserved it. But if we had wanted to, we could have sold our shares for very much more.

Not bad for a couple of immigrants.

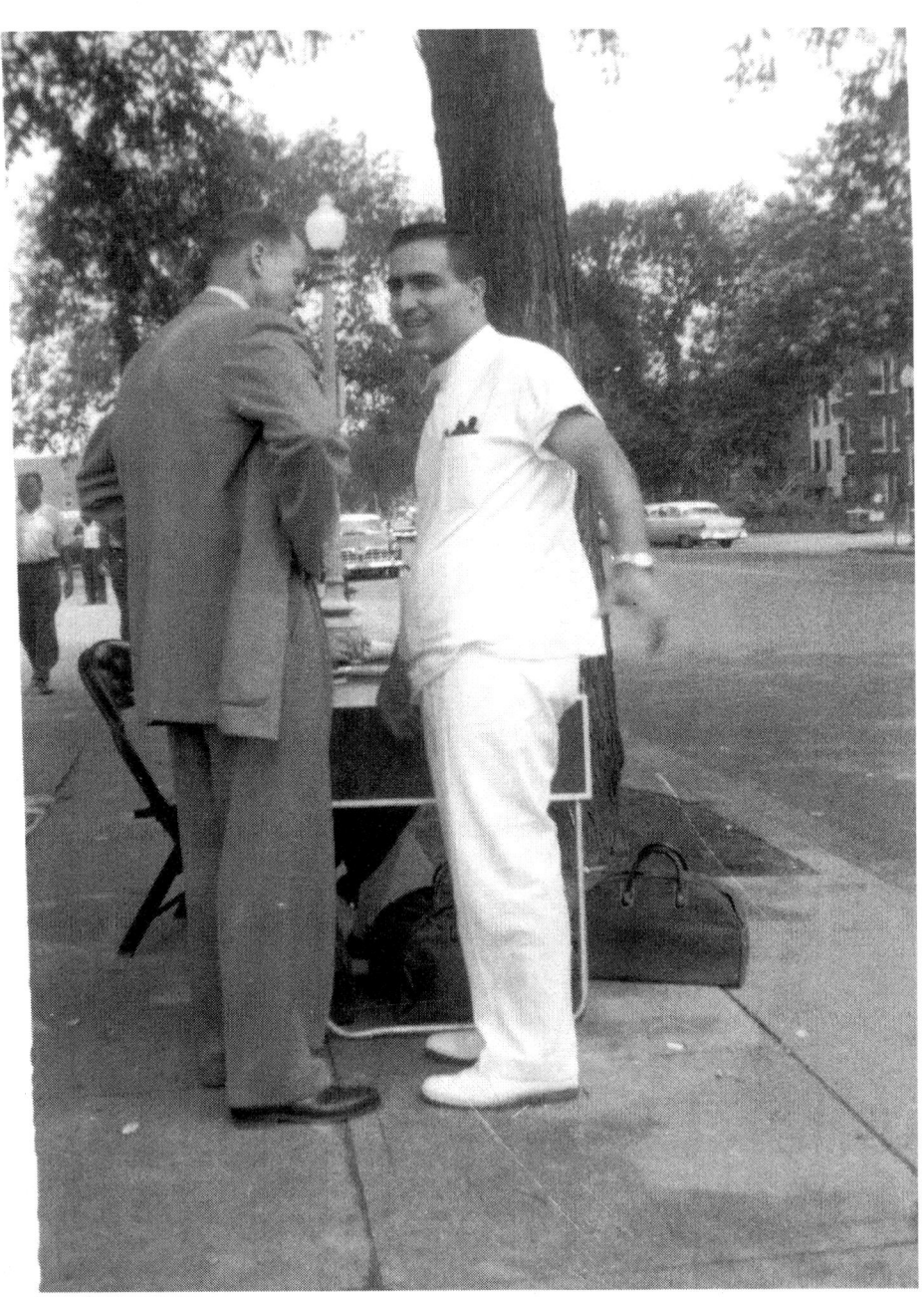

Dr. Jim drawing blood on the streets of Washington, D.C.

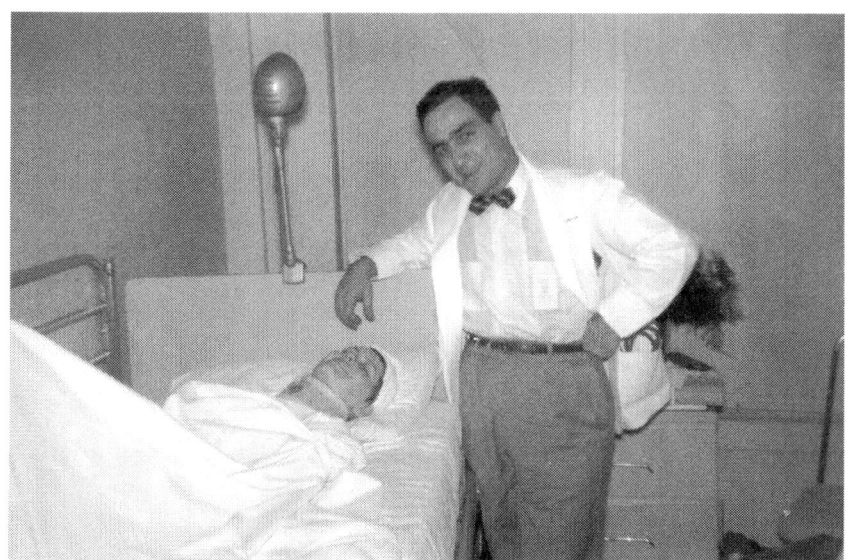

Dr. Jim with patient

Darla's friend, Darla and Dr. Jim

Darla and Dr. Jim

Dr. Jim

Dr. Jim, Darla inside car

Dr. Jim and Darla dancing

Dr. Jim and Dr. George – City Hall – Utah

Dr. Jim in Residency – University of Utah

Darla and Dr. Jim on Wedding Day

Dr. George Farha   **Dr. Jim Farha**

Palm Sunday with Dr. George and Dr. Jim's children
Dr. Jim holding Tiffany, Maria, Gayle (behind Maria), Joan, Laura, Julie,
Brenda, Darla holding Todd, Mark (in front)

Chapter 13: Darla's Family

Working so desperately for a goal you've been trying to achieve basically your entire life can blind you to the things going on around you. I missed a lot of activities with my kids, especially the less important ones, like sending them off to church when I was too busy to attend myself. True to our agreement to raise the children in my religion, I took the kids to Sunday School at the Orthodox church in town. I'd go see a few patients while they were there, and then I'd be back around to pick them up. I often didn't have time to go myself, so I didn't realize what a lousy preacher we had. I was much more interested in keeping my practice going. It only came to my attention when the priest was fired years later. It was a big scandal, because it's very rare that a priest disrobes.

But Darla noticed the problem long before the priest was fired. She would ask the kids what they learned at Sunday School, and they would answer, "We just colored." It concerned her, and she brought up that concern with me. She wanted our children to actually be learning something when they went to church. Knowing the Mormon Church in our area had better programs, she asked me if it would be alright if she took them to Sunday School with her every once in a while.

Although Darla was a very strong Mormon, we didn't practice the faith in our home. I was very attached to the old tradition, and I wanted our home to be as Orthodox Christian as it could. But I didn't see the harm in the children going to church with their mother every once in a while. So I gave my consent and continued to go about my business.

After a little while of attending that church, Maria and Tiffany decided that they wanted to be baptized into that Church. It came as a shock to me, and there was quite a bit of discomfort in the house for a long period of time when Darla and I worked through it. I was angry that Darla had put her religion before my culture. But Darla wasn't rubbing it in my face, and she was very sensitive to my feelings and opinions. Even when we were arguing, she kept a great demeanor and a great attitude, unlike myself, and it really is because of her that we didn't get divorced. And although I've never been able to forget, I have since forgiven. Darla was such a good wife, a good mother, a good person over all that it wasn't that hard for her to gain my forgiveness. It was somewhat my fault, anyway. I was guilty in the sense that I left the opportunity wide open. If I wanted things to be run my way, I should have done a better job running them.

Neither of my boys ended up joining the church, but both of my girls did. One of them even served a mission after college. Maria was attending Southern Methodist University, a school her mother and I had helped to pick out, and after the first semester she decided she didn't like it there very much. Darla, ever sensitive to meet the needs of her children, arranged to have her go to BYU instead. It was very difficult to get into BYU at that time, but Darla was influential in the church, especially the local congregation. Like I said before, everybody who knew Darla loved her. So our daughter got in, attended, and was converted to the faith, being baptized and everything. She liked it so much that she decided to volunteer her time to it. She was called to serve a mission to France. I was a little miffed that I had to pay to send my daughter on a mission that I didn't believe in. But in the end, I wanted to do what would make her happy, and her happiness was worth a little bit of cash going to a church I wasn't a member of.

One of the good things about having children in the Mormon Church is that it is a church that instills good family values into its members. I have two sons-in-law who are Mormon, and I love both of them. They are good people and they are very good fathers, probably better parents than I was. I was too preoccupied to be the kind of father they both are; I left raising the children to Darla. (And she did a great job, too—you don't get four kids like mine by accident.) But my two sons-in-law concentrate a lot of family time and family values and because of that they've raised good families.

But not being a member of the Mormon Church sometimes kept me from closer relationships with my family, especially my extended family. I got along well enough with Darla's family; I liked them and respected who they were and what they believed. And I enjoyed going to family gatherings—really enjoyed them, although it was also a good way to please Darla—but the conversation was always centered on the church. I sometimes felt I was outside the conversation. There were so many other things we could have, and sometimes did, talked about (politics, national events, sports), but for some reason the conversation always came back around to church subjects. I just wasn't interested in the individuals in the church they talked about, so I was not always involved in their conversations and that was hard for me sometimes.

Despite any differences we may have had, I really did enjoy Darla's family. They were hard working people although they were not very educated themselves. Darla's mother was the smart one, a businesswoman who didn't have a degree. Her father was a simple man who didn't study beyond high school. But they both emphasized Darla's education in her own life, which translated to our children. Each of our children became very successful not only in their personal endeavors but also just as human beings within their community. And a lot of that came back to the values Darla learned from her parents. Although I may have been the son-in-law they didn't want, they were always civil toward me.

Darla's parents met when her father was on a mission to Vienna, Austria. My mother-in-law was a foreigner much like me. So we got along really well. She really was a wonderful lady. She always stayed with Darla for a few days when a new baby was born to us, to help her get adjusted to the change. I remember vividly one particular instance. She had just finished her stay to help take care of one of the kids, and she was packed and ready to leave. But the very day she would have gone back home, she developed a blockage of the artery in her leg, which was a very serious condition. And unfortunately all of the members of the group who dealt with that sort of thing were out of town. It's often very difficult to operate on someone you are emotionally close to. I didn't want to operate on her, but I had to. She insisted that I do it, and we did it under local anesthesia so that she could leave as soon as she could to head home. Fortunately everything went well.

Unfortunately she was mismanaged. We weren't very knowledgeable in those days, and she had a condition that we didn't know too much about. It was unfortunate; had she received proper management, she would have lived to be an old lady, but instead she died in her sixties. I enjoyed her immensely, and I've missed her a lot since she passed.

When she passed, I discovered that she had written me into her will as the executor of her estate. She had four children she could have selected, but she chose me instead. It showed me that she not only cared about me but trusted me, too. She saw that I was apt at managing my own money and she knew I'd do a good job at managing hers.

Chapter 14: Making Wichita Home

Darla loved to renovate and decorate houses. We didn't have much to work with in Utah—just the shabby apartment that she did her best to light up. In Wichita, with Maria already born and Mark S. on the way, Darla and I thought it would be better for us to rent a house rather than rent another apartment. We had already decided that we didn't want to live on the west side—or at least George didn't think that we should. So, still living out of George's basement, we decided to scour the east side neighborhoods to find a house with a "For Rent" sign.

After looking for a while, we found a nice house that we really liked. It was a great house with several bedrooms and it came fully furnished with all new furniture. The only problem was that it was for sale, not for rent. We didn't have the money to be able to afford it, so we decided to take a look to see who the owner was. It was owned by Jon Kardatzke, but he was in the military and his father, Reverend Kardatzke, was the one managing it while he was gone. He was a preacher in the First Church of God. Later, I would learn to admire him a great deal.

I went to Reverend Kardatzke to see if there was any possible way we could rent the house from him. Seeing that I was a young married man, he asked if I had any children. When I answered that I did, he immediately turned down the deal.

"We tried renting it out before," he explained to me. "But the last time didn't go so well. They devastated the house and the furniture. So we've decided we aren't going to rent it anymore."

I was disappointed, but I understood. I thanked him for his time, intending to end the conversation. Before I could go, though, he threw in a final question. "By the way, what's your name?"

"Jim Farha," I answered. "I'm a new physician in town."

Surprisingly, that sparked some recognition in him. "Oh, a Farha? Do you know William Farha?"

"Of course!" I answered, "He's one of my uncles." We got to talking about William for a little bit, and that seemed to change the Reverend's mind.

"If William's your uncle, you've got to be a good person. I'll let you rent the house." He set the terms at around $125 a month. I told him I would be willing to pay that amount if I could, but that I really just couldn't afford it.

"Do you think you can accept $90 a month?" I asked hopefully.

Luckily he said yes and Darla, Maria, and I were able to move in. We maintained the house very well and the Reverend and I maintained a good relationship after that. He introduced me to his sons—Stan, who was a physician, and Jon, when he got back from serving in the military—and from that our families forged a tremendous relationship. I remember the days when Stan and I were both raising our young daughters at the same time. We were both so broke that we'd set our girls up on a play date together and share the cost of a babysitter when we wanted to go out. Over time, as the family practice grew and the Kardatzke's began their own businesses, our friendly relationship grew into a really big business relationship that we all benefited from. And it all started with a house rental.

After we rented from the Kardatzke's for a while, we bought our first house in Wichita, on Pine Crest, in 1966. I insisted that I did not want to spend more than $12,000 on a house. I wasn't used to borrowing money, and I didn't want to borrow a large amount. But George smiled at me and said, "There's no way you can get a decent house for $12,000." He insisted that we buy a house on the east side, and I am grateful for that, because we located a house in a decent neighborhood. I think it was something like 3,000 square feet for $34,000.

I wasn't sure at first how I was going to pay for it. But my cousin Philip Farha owned the savings and loan, so we let him take care of it. He went and saw the house, called me, and said, "You just bought a house." We still didn't have much by the way of money at that point and we couldn't pay a down payment, so the mortgage payments were really high, about $800 a month. Although it made me uncomfortable, we were committed. I'd earn the money somehow; the payments weren't going to pay themselves. There was nothing else we could do.

I took care of the lawn and planted trees and Darla painted the inside. We took George's couch from his basement—it was a nice little couch. We had a bed that Darla's mother sent us; that was a great, nice antique bed. The rest of our furniture was from Salvation Army, including the bunk beds. Darla was a great shopper. She knew how to select quality things. As a matter of fact, one of the tables from Salvation Army is still in my basement in Wichita, many years later.

We sold our house on Pine Crest a few years later to be closer to George. Our second house was at Second and Terrace, caddy corner from George's house. It was a very big, old house, built around 1930. And it was gorgeous. Darla had a field day with it—finally she had something to use her talents on. She redid the entire thing and we loved living there. But we didn't live there for very long. We were on a busy street and we kept losing dogs to traffic, which was heartbreaking for us and especially for the kids. Darla decided that she wanted to move out to the country. And Darla had a way of using her charm to get what she wanted (she knew I was captivated by her), so that's what we did.

We located a farm with eighty acres on which sat a three thousand square foot home. The home itself was fairly modern, and the land had stables for horses and hay barns and pretty white pipe fencing. When we first made an offer on the property, we thought everything was settled. But then the owner, a prominent and well-respected oil man, came to me and said, "Look, I'm sick, and I want to move into the city as soon as possible to be close to a hospital. Why don't you move into my house, and I'll move into yours, and we'll let the lawyers take care of it later?" I thought it was a fine idea, so we sealed the deal with a handshake and we switched houses. Then I called the lawyers and told them to take care of it.

My lawyer was shocked and perhaps a little annoyed. "Don't tell me you already moved without signing any papers!" he said to me.

"That's right. I did. He's living in my house now."

To my lawyer's surprise, it all worked out very well. We got the papers drawn up and signed everything appropriately without a problem.

We all liked living on the farm a lot. It was a ball, and we made lasting memories there. I bought the kids go-carts and let the grass in the backyard grow until they had a nice racetrack to race on. They spent hours racing each other in the backyard. Maria started a horseback teaching school once she was old enough and had enough training. She made good money from that, and had no overhead to offset. She ended up saving enough to make a trip to Europe.

Darla worked her decorating magic on that house, too. By the time she was finished, it was between seven and eight thousand square feet, more than twice the size it was when we bought it. She put a basement under part of it, and added a swimming pool and a lagoon (which was necessary, since there was no sewage system). She did basically all of it herself—all the negotiating and managing, and everything built to code— since I wasn't around much. All I really did to help was sign the checks.

I went to work early in the morning and came home between eight and ten o'clock at night—when I was in town I was always available to my patients. But I made a little time on the weekends to help work the land. I bought an old tractor and a new tractor and I called myself a gentleman farmer. Todd, who was probably between seven and ten at the time we were making changes, helped me with the work. We "built" roads and planted a lot of trees. He enjoyed the work. Mark participated, too, but he didn't like it very much.

We had a ball at the farm. It's where my kids grew up and it contains a lot of really good memories for us. If we had had the energy and the means to maintain it, we probably would have continued staying there for the rest of our lives, but many things changed.

* * *

Darla was a great contributor in every aspect of our lives. Being an essentially absent father, Darla took care of the day-to-day decisions and she really was the one who raised our kids to be such outstanding people. She was a miracle worker, and it really astounded me that she was able to accomplish so much. Not only did she do so much for our family around the house but she also did a lot to help me in my practice referrals.

She and Brenda, George's wife, did a lot to help keep up the relationships we had with our referring physicians. I don't know how George and I could have run our practices without them. They spent hours making gifts and visiting physician's practices. They also cooked numerous dinners so that we could host those very same physicians in our homes. And they cooked numerous dinners for the young members of our surgical group. The senior members developed a tradition of treating the young members and their families, and their extended families if they came to down, with a good deal of old-fashioned hospitality. If we didn't have our wives, we wouldn't have been able to keep up with it all.

They were also the ones who executed George's Christmas idea that has turned into a tradition that has become one of my very favorites. We used to go Christmas caroling with our surgical group (even though I still hadn't mastered all the carols in English). We'd rent one or two buses and go visit some of the physicians at their homes, as well as a few personal friends' homes, and we'd stop the tour at George and Brenda's home. There we would have chili and hot drinks, enjoying each other's company and generally becoming closer to each other. It really helped to foster camaraderie and unity within the group.

Darla began another tradition that still stands to this day: Christmas Eve at Dr. Jim's house. We like to make a great big deal of it. We decorate the house with lights and make sure to put up a great big tree. We hire a pianist to provide background music and accompany us when we sing Christmas carols. We have a caterer provide food, both Lebanese and American, so there's something for everybody.

The main event is the nativity story, which the kids act out. When my kids were young, they were the ones acting it out with their cousins, playing all the important parts. Now that they're older, they compete over whose baby gets to play Jesus each year! It really is quite a great show, and I think everybody has a good time.

And by everybody I do mean everybody. Many of our friends and family know about it and turn up every year, even without an invitation. We expect immediate members of the family, extended members of the family, friends, members of the group and their family, neighbors, you name it. We probably average hosting one hundred or more people each year. I wouldn't trade the memories of it for anything.

* * *

After George and I settled into our practice we decided we had to send a certain amount of money to my parents. I didn't have any money of my own at the time, but we borrowed $20,000 from the bank (George showed me how) and we sent a certain amount to them every month. I remember my parents arguing about how the money should be spent, because Mother would want to spend some money on a new dress, and Father wanted to save that money for more important reasons. He was a very wise and generous man. My father never used that money on himself. He always used it to help some of his daughters and their children. I think he regretted not being able to spend money on his other six children's education. He focused a lot on helping George and me, and he wanted to be able to help his other children, too.

We also decided that since we could afford it, we would go back and visit our parents once every year. We took our entire family along—wife, kids, even a few times with kids on the way. We alternated years so that my parents got a visit each year. We didn't feel that we could each reasonably spend the time and money to go once a year. As a surgeon, if you are on vacation, you don't have an income for that time period. Although we were making good money, we both had some insecurity about our finances because of our upbringing in the depression, where we had nothing. We had food, we had lots of grain, we had farming products that came from Palestine, but we had very little, and there're certain things you just don't forget.

As if we needed it, visiting the old country with our families was another reminder that Wichita really was our true home. Coming to America at such a young age really affected who I was, how I felt and how I thought. I appreciated the new system, the new thinking, the new philosophy. I felt very much a foreigner in Lebanon, mostly because I was not in the mainstream culturally there.

I took my kids to the old country, to the little town where I grew up. Everything looked so small, and it was all neglected. There had been an Israel occupation of Southern Lebanon and everything was disrupted. Many people had simply left their homes to fall apart. I felt very uncomfortable there; we stayed for only one night and left the next day to head back to Beirut. At least there was an American embassy there and you were close to the airport.

George and I had the most amazing wives. George had married a Farha, a distant cousin, named Brenda. And we all know Darla and how amazing she was. But each year either Darla or Brenda with their kids went to Lebanon ahead of us. Which meant they were traveling alone to a very foreign country without the help of their husbands. We needed the extra time with our practices, and our kids needed the extra time getting to know their grandparents. For our first few visits, we stayed with my parents in their home, as was the custom. It was not normal for visitors to stay at a hotel when family was around. But their apartment had maybe two or three bedrooms and a single bathroom, and as our families grew, it started to become very uncomfortable and inconvenient, especially since we were used to the space that our homes in America afforded us. Eventually we started staying in a hotel when we came to visit.

In Beirut, you don't find houses with a lawn or grass or anything like that. My parents were living in a high-rise building that had a tiny supermarket at the bottom. Most apartments are set up that way—they have a shop with everything you would need in it, but not much else. Each building has its own world, being on its own electric grid with a generator. The water or the electricity would die some of the time. Knowing what sort of benefits you'd be getting at the apartment was very unpredictable, and George and I knew that we could help them to afford something much better. So we decided to buy them a new place. A house this time, much nicer and much bigger.

When my father found out what we were doing, he was upset with us. He didn't want to move; he thought his apartment was very adequate. What he wanted was the money back. We'd depleted his money. Mother said not to give him the money. If we gave it to him, she insisted, they would never move and he would spend all the cash on extended responsibilities. She was excited at the prospect of living in a nicer place, and she supported our efforts to move them.

In George's wisdom, he proposed that we each fund half of the endeavor. We transferred about $20,000 through Chase–Manhattan to the branch in Beirut, which for one of the first times in our life, didn't seem like an overwhelmingly large amount of money. It was an easy transfer, and it felt good to finally be giving something substantial back to my parents.

I located the place we wanted for our parents to move to. It was a very nice house with a clear title and a willing seller. There shouldn't have been any issues with it. The man with the cash wrote a check for it, verifiable in an instant. But we were told that it would take two or three months to process the paperwork. It would take many weeks and we only had a few!

So we started looking around for help. A distant relative of ours was a Lebanese Congressman, and we asked him if he could help us out. He said he would, but he told us to bring a lot of cash in loose change. The people who could get the job done for us wanted some "good will" from us. I was really embarrassed that it had to work out that way. You're essentially paying them to move the envelope from one desk to another in the same office. But it was the only way to get it done in a week and be able to go back home and get back to work. Fortunately, with the help of a congressman (Mr. Samara) and multiple "good wills", we were able to make the deal in a week or so. That gave us just a few days to furnish it.

In Beirut, you can't just open the yellow pages and see a list of furniture stores. You have to go out and find them, and it's very disorganized (at least for my American thinking). I found it very difficult driving all over the city trying to find the right stuff in the right stores. And my wife was five or six months pregnant with Todd at the time. She was a trooper.

However, I think for Darla the most frustrating thing was not being able to find a clothes dryer. She really wanted my parents to have a washer and dryer, if only for the times when we would come to visit. We went from store to store asking if they had one, but no one had what Darla had in mind. They had a clothes washer, alright, and it would wash your clothes and spin them dry, but they weren't meant to be used as a dryer like we have in America. They just don't sell dryers there. That's not how you do laundry in the old country. If you need something dried, what's wrong with the sun?

She also got a little scared sometimes that my nephews were going to get in a fist fight. In Lebanon, you don't go into a store, ask how much a product costs, and buy it at face value. You bargain for things. You might go into a store and buy a one-hundred-dollar table for ten bucks. But it's not the easiest thing to do, or to witness, if you are generally an amiable, non-confrontational person like my wife was. You get right into each other's faces and argue. You shout and you swear on your mother's grave or God or whatever you swear on that you are losing money in the deal. I found it unpleasant, but I knew that it was just how the game was played. It had been a while since I had done that sort of bargaining, and I didn't like it much, so I had my nephews help. They were almost as old as I am, but they knew the game. My nephew Ghassen did especially well with such things. They told me to just be quiet, so I was. They got great deals on the furniture for our parents and afterwards, they shook hands with the sellers and had coffee and everybody was happy.

After a few days of hunting, we furnished the house and got them moved in. My older brother Fayez helped a great deal with the move. We took care of everything, and my parents were able to live out the rest of their lives in that house rent-free.

Shopping in Lebanon was a most unusual experience to me. Although I grew up but there I never had the experience of shopping there. The negotiation was very intense and appeared to be full of anger but always ended up with a handshake and a smile. Many of my nephews helped us in the process but Ghassan, Ghaleb and Herta were at the forefront. Mother loved flowers and Darla knew that. We spent hours looking for a cement, wide basin and the appropriate flowers so that Mother would feel at home.

All trips to Lebanon were great joy. I cannot name all the relatives and friends who made our visits most joyous. Most impressive to me was the trip to Marjeyoun which always looked absolutely beautiful.

Chapter 15: Other Ventures in Wichita

Once George and I had established ourselves, we decided it was time to bring our family to Wichita as well. It was George's idea, really. One day, George came to me and said, "You know, we oughtta bring Violette and Shafeek to Wichita from Virginia." They were a great couple, and Violette had been so close to George and me while we were growing up.

George and I thanked God for Violette and Shafeek, because we never would have been allowed to come to American without their influence. They really did a lot to help us get settled when we made our own move to America, and all that time in Virginia really helped us to become closer to them than we were any of our other siblings. We wanted to return the favor, but I felt a little trepidation at the prospect of moving them and their four kids all the way out to Kansas. Both of them had established businesses and we were concerned that they wouldn't be able to succeed as well in a city that was much larger than Pulaski, West Virginia, but finally everyone agreed.

"That's a big move," I said. "They have a family and a business they'd have to bring along." They ran a store in Pulaski, and Violette would not give it up easily.

"We'll work it out." George said. He seemed determined. And where there's a will, there's a way.

Luckily with all the family and friends in Wichita already forming a pretty solid support group, it wasn't too difficult to move them in. Besides, Violette had already been through a lot and knew how to handle herself. When she first came to America, she and her husband lived with her in-laws in one bedroom, which is a difficult situation for any married couple. Finally she insisted that they move out, which they did, taking residence in Pulaski, where they worked hard to establish their business.

They worked just as hard in Wichita as they did in Pulaski, opening a very classy designer woman's clothing store. It didn't pay much, but it made them a living and the good Lord took care of everything else. When they first came, they could only afford to rent a small house, but that didn't stop Violette's big heart. They were always very jovial, a great addition to our blood-related family as well as the family of Lebanese immigrants we'd come to love so much. They loved every minute of Violette's life there. She'd have everybody—all of my kids, all of George's kids, all of the grandkids when they came— over to her house every single Sunday for a great big meal. It was something everyone looked forward to. She was just a magnificent woman. I must add that in my humble opinion she was the most efficient woman I've ever known and I loved her for it.

It turns out we didn't need to worry about how her kids would adjust, either, because each of them benefitted (and I would even go far as to say benefitted greatly) from coming to Wichita. They all have done well, some a bit better than others. For instance, one of her children is a vascular surgeon; he's the one who took over as head of the group when George and I retired. On top of that, he's a professor, chair of the department of surgery, and the director of the surgical training program. He wears many hats, and he wears them well. Alex Ammar is truly a wonderful doctor, great leader and very achievement oriented. He has lead the group of WSS very successfully, and leading doctors is as hard as herding cats. He has executed this in a truly exceptional fashion.

George and I also helped Georgette and her husband, Adib find their way to Wichita, too. They had been in America for some time, thanks to a relative in Houston, but didn't move out to Wichita for a few years. I'm unsure of the details on how they arrived in America or how they got to Wichita, but I know that one of her sons was instrumental in the process. He now has a PhD in software and hardware and has done exceptionally well. He really is a genius with tech. He and his brothers went along to create a high-tech company that George and I helped fund at its inception. They were all really exceptional boys, exceptional Americans, who did extremely well in their careers. Alif, Elias and Basil have been a great addition to Wichita and to our family.

When we brought Fayez over, I think it was his son who made the application to come over. Fayez had escaped the war with his family, lived in Saudi Arabia with his son in a two-bedroom apartment, then went to Egypt. But he had no income, so they were put on a waiting list. Immigration was different back then; if you had a sponsor, it was a lot easier to come in. So George and I offered some financial help and were helpful in bringing him over to Wichita. Eventually his sons came along to Wichita as well. Adib was a wonderful help to his entire family and has worked hard to achieve that.

Fayez was in poor health when he came to America, and that hindered him a lot in obtaining his American citizenship. Every time he was scheduled to go to the courthouse to be sworn in as an American citizen, he was too sick to go. But he loved America and he really wanted to become a citizen, so he pleaded with me and George to find a way to get him his citizenship, whether he was sick or not. We couldn't just set another court date because we couldn't count on him being healthy when it came around. But there was a federal judge, Judge Kelly, in Wichita who I had some connections with. Before he was a judge, he was an attorney, and he was representing a man on whom I'd performed surgery. The man had been in a serious car accident. He maintained a lot of damage—he lost an eye and had multiple fractures. His wife even lost an arm. I was called as an expert witness, and I testified to the truth, which made the judge a lot of money. He was a great American and a good human being with a lot of empathy.

But Judge Kelly was a big shot judge now. He was involved

in protecting an abortion clinic with the sheriff, and he was well-known and highly respected. We decided it wouldn't hurt to see if Judge Kelly could help us out. We called his office and told him my brother was anxious to be a citizen. He told us he'd see what he could do. We weren't expecting much, maybe just for Faiyez to be listed for a few separate dates to keep his schedule more flexible. But the judge called one day with a big surprise. He was going to stop by Fayez's house and swear him in personally. That really made an impact on George and me. He was a very busy and important man, and it touched us that he was so willing to help out an average Joe to fulfill a dream.

Violette, Georgette, and Fayez were the only ones George and I were able to bring to Wichita. Our other siblings were too old. Suad Shdeed came to visit multiple times but ultimately decided to go back; we didn't get to spend much time with her after that because she died relatively young. But it really was a great thing to have the financial stability of a career you'd built up as well as the emotional stability of a family who surrounded you and loved you.

And just think of the siblings we brought—the great majority of them have been contributors to society. We are all tangible proof that immigrants who come to this country with a little fire in the belly are able to get places. The members of my family employed hundreds, maybe more, of people and created companies that became public. They contributed a lot to society. And it's because none of us were complacent. We didn't expect any handouts. We didn't need a "nanny government", we just needed a government to protect our rights and give us the opportunity to follow our passions.

Coming to America is the most wonderful thing that's happened to me. I couldn't have accomplished what I was able to accomplish here anywhere else. George and I could have made it in Lebanon had we come back after getting our degrees, that's for sure. There are a lot of educated doctors who survived there, and we were both ambitious enough that we could have made it work. But there's no way we could have helped so many people, made so many innovations, hired so many people, or taken so many business risks in Lebanon. There just wasn't the freedom for it.

George and I came as a couple of foreigners. We were very different. But we overcame any fear or uneasiness and we tried to insinuate ourselves into various aspects of society. We wanted to really be a part of it, to contribute. We wanted to be proud of wherever we were—it was our community after all. And now Wichita is home, not Lebanon. There's no other country that treats its immigrants like America does. All in all, this is God's country.

All immigrants might have similar opportunities as us, but not all immigrants experience the limited success that George and I did. We were very lucky in our careers and in our connections. Although practicing medicine gave me and my family a comfortable living, I really gained my stability through business investments.

Before I started any of my own investing, Darla did some. She was so bright. She went to an auction and bought a farm that we sold seven or eight years later for maybe twenty times what we paid for it. I remember her calling me when I was in surgery and I said, "Look, I don't have time to visit."

"No," she informed me. "I just want you to find $10,000. I just wrote a check for $10,000."

I finished the case I was doing and I called her and said, "What are you doing?"

She said, "I just bought the whole farm, 160 acres." I had only authorized her to buy forty, the front forty. But she thought it was cheap enough, and it turns out she was right.

I rushed to the bank. I introduced myself. I had no money. They asked who I knew in town and I said, "I know my brother George Farha. I know William Farha, I know all the Farhas." They checked me out. They loaned me the $10,000, and they mortgaged the farm for the rest, and that was a bonanza. After that, we went on to explore and invest in every little thing that came our way.

George and I were both very busy as surgeons, but we knew that investing was a very important aspect of accumulating wealth, so we made time for other business. We were always silent partners so we could make the most of our investments without spending more time than was necessary to fulfill our responsibilities. We used to conduct our business at night or on the weekend or whenever we had the time. And we were both successful in alternative business approaches—once we figured out what we were doing at least.

Getting involved with business ventures was another testament to me that you learn a hell of a lot more from failures than you do successes. When George and I first started out, our investments were all over the place. We went in with a group of dry cleaners, which was a total loss. We tried going in with a video business next, which was also a total loss. Then we tried a recycling company, which was also a total loss! We probably invested in about ten start-up companies overall, but only two or three of them actually made it. And that was only after we finally realized that the best way to see success was to invest in what we knew.

We had a good income and a good signature, so borrowing money was not a problem. But we only made returns on our money when we invested in or attempted to nurture a health care issue. You should not pour your faith, or your cash, into something that you don't really understand. The regulatory business was also much easier with healthcare businesses than with the others we tried to jump start. The greatest element in building a successful business is Liberty. Free people can innovate, produce and be self-dependent and can achieve success.

Our first venture, started by Stan Kardatzke, was called Health Care Plus. It must have been one of the first Health Maintenance Organizations to set up shop in the West in the late seventies. It was a small company, but together George and I owned a high percentage of it. The whole concept of having HMOs doesn't help surgeons much. It's a gatekeeper concept. A doctor will get a certain number of dollars to spend to take care (per family) of his patients. And the only way the patient will get to see a specialty doctor (like a surgeon) is if the general doctor refers him or her and has the money to pay for it. Unfortunately, once the money got into the doctor's account, he felt that it was his, and sometimes, a doctor might withhold care. If he says the patient shouldn't have heart surgery, then the patient wouldn't have heart surgery. So it wasn't the best business concept for a surgeon. But the general practitioners would get more clients that way because the HMOs could offer lower insurance premiums. And that was a good business concept for an investor. So George and I followed the business, feeling it was a good idea to invest with the general practitioners. We had a great relationship with the family doctors, anyway, so even after the HMO took off we still got referrals from them.

We didn't invest a whole lot of money into the business, but we got almost twenty times what we put in by the time we pulled out of it. George was a little more invested than I was; he was even on their board at some point, I think. But it turned out to be a very successful endeavor and we were glad we took the risk. The company went on to be sold to the Hospital Corporation of America (HCA), who afterwards sold it to Humana. The trust and good faith that we had built with all physicians, in particular the Family Practice doctors, enabled us to participate in certain health care investments.

As we were selling our shares in Health Care Plus, we had a little extra cash. Stan Kardatzke, a good friend of mine in town, was its chairman and got to talking to us about it. He complimented us on the great job we had done and let us in on a little secret. He had been to a meeting with the HCA and heard that they might be moving to Wichita. The idea of HCA was to have a hospital without borders and with a very broad network. Their doctors would function solely under HCA and would refer patients solely to HCA-owned hospitals. It is a generous concept, but if it works it can be really lucrative.

I got the idea to piggyback on the HCA idea. We could create a PCA (Physicians Clinic of America) and put PCA clinics next to every HCA hospital. It would be a clinic without borders. I thought it was a great idea: they'd rhyme, they'd be side-by-side, and the idea could easily extend to other HCA hospitals throughout the nation. And not only that—we'd be able to control healthcare delivery in the proper way. I've always thought there's a lot of waste in medicine, and we'd be able to fix that problem in a big way.

Just as Stan predicted, HCA came to Wichita. They bought Wesley Medical Center from another company, and it became the biggest hospital they owned at the time. I shared my idea with Stan, who loved it too, and we got a few other doctors on board (Bill Loewen, Jon Kardatzke, and others). We each invested a significant sum of money to create an infrastructure. We developed high-tech communication to use between the clinics, built a laboratory, and made contracts with the hospitals. Then we started to buy family doctors' practices, first in Wichita and quickly extending outside of Wichita and throughout the rest of Kansas. We promoted the idea however we could. I was a busy surgeon so I promoted it only by visiting with some other doctors. I had a pretty good name, though, and I really believed in the product, so others trusted me and got on board, too. Soon we had a very large number of physicians and we even tried outside the state. It seemed to us that the concept was working very well; there were no boundaries. According to Stan, we were also earning a penny a share, which he thought was great. We were on the way to success.

But once again my compulsion blinded me. I really, honestly believed in the concept and I really wanted to see it succeed, but I was busy and I didn't see the problem when it emerged and couldn't do anything about it when it became prominent. Unfortunately, there was some sort of dissention within the group and it started to fall apart from the inside out. We had a good relationship, and were working predominately with, Wesley hospital (because it was an HCA institution at that point), but some meddlesome relationship between the hospital administration and our own leadership broke the bond our companies had and the company began to falter. Stan and I started considering our options for exiting the company.

The two guys who engineered the survival of the company

as it stands today were Dr. George and another George, George Ablah. The only way to salvage the company was to have the physicians take ownership, which created a lot of legal issues that I won't go into, or to sell the clinic to a hospital. It seemed easier to sell it to a hospital, especially if we played our cards right. Most of the hospitals in Wichita have grown from their original size into larger structures with misshapen appendages as the need warranted it. It's inefficient. So we proposed building a state-of-the-art high-rise hospital. It wouldn't need to be expanded, it would be built with all the necessaries built in. I don't know whether it was pretend or whether we were really serious about the project, but we put some serious thought and marketing into it.

They presented to St. Francis and pressured them until they bought the "Clinic without Walls," the PCK for around twelve million dollars. However, walls were put around the clinic deliberately and we changed the name to the Physicians Clinic of Kansas (PCK). It was a byproduct of the PCA concept.

At this point I stepped out of my active role in the company because my practice was hurting. I still had a lot of shares in the PCA as a whole, and I was putting quite a few of them into my kids' trust funds, but I couldn't have my name associated with it in Wichita. A lot of private doctors didn't like the PCA and they stopped sending me, and other people in my surgical group, referrals. So I stepped out to repair the damage.

Dr. George, George and other important members took the money they got from St. Francis and bought a privately owned HMO in Miami. I was told it was mismanaged but they were going to clean it up once they were managing it. They turned this new organization into a branch of PCA, and it began to do very well again. The organization was strictly "Medicaid," and the governor of Florida, Governor Childes, declared that the providers for Medicaid patients should be paid at private insurance levels. After that, PCA's earnings went way up and the company went public. I started selling my shares soon after that—one bird in the hand is better than ten on the tree—and my kids and I all benefited significantly from selling our shares on the open market.

So I was completely out of the PCA loop when it took its next blow. The PCA bought a company that was predominantly involved in workers' compensation, and it had a lot of issues. The reputation and the trust in the PCA name went down significantly, really depressing the company. At one point the shares were worth forty or fifty dollars each, but Humana bought PCA for only six dollars a share. When the price of the shares dropped, I bought a few, because I thought it was still a good company and I didn't know the shakiness that existed because of the workers' compensation problems. Although I didn't get any returns from the investments that time around, my returns from previous investments were enough to pay for my retirement and for the kids to have full trust funds.

The Kardatzke's and I continued to be business partners for a few more projects after that. They were doing very well for themselves. Their group grew to become a very large family practice group. It was probably the best and biggest in the west portion of Wichita. I think it was called West Side Family Practice. At one point it had probably thirty primary care physicians in it, and it went on to be managed by a very capable family doctor: Dr. William Loewen.

But the family practice wasn't the only good idea the Kardatzke's had. They asked us to be silent partners when they started a nursing home on the west side of the city. I would own about twenty percent. I didn't know much about the details of how it would be run or the structure of the company, but I trusted their business sense enough to invest. I borrowed $4,500 dollars to make an investment. It became a huge complex, enlarging to become an almost full-service nursing center. You'd push a button, you'd get a nurse. It was a great idea and it grew quickly. It was making me quite a bit of money. I was paying seventy percent of it to Uncle Sam, though, so I gave a bunch to my kids so they could get a share of the returns.

Stan Kardatzke was an absolute genius in many ways and had so many ideas; however, his management style at times was not as good as his visionary component. I enjoyed a very close relationship with him and unfortunately and sadly he died at a relatively young age.

Chapter 16: Retirement

I never used drugs, and I've never abused any substance. I drank a little scotch or a little wine here and there, but I was never a heavy drinker. I smoked for much of my early life, but I quit smoking many times, usually for eight or ten months. Then I'd weaken and get back onto them. The last time I quit was around 1985, and it was permanent. I haven't always gotten enough rest, thanks to being overworked, and I often didn't have time to really care about watching my diet and exercising regularly. Looking back on my life and knowing what I know now, my health problems must have started very early, probably when I was around forty or fifty years old.

Around 1992, I was diagnosed with heart disease.

I had known for a little while that something was wrong. I had had episodes where I thought I was hyperventilating, and it turns out I was actually having angina, which is associated with coronary artery disease. It is often manifested as shortness of breath. My health was deteriorating rapidly and I thought I was on my way out. My coronary artery disease was severe, and I'd never done anything to treat it. I was getting older, anyway, and I figured the sooner I got out, the better. There was no point to keep on pushing if it was only going to kill me.

George was getting tired, too. And so around the year 1999, we had both retired and that's when we sold the group. We never interfered with it once we left. We didn't even own any shares in it. Now the only thing I have left of the group is a pen that says WSS on it. Sometimes I wonder if we could have structured the move a little better than simply walking away and hoping that leadership kept on how you thought it should. You have to remember these are forty very different surgeons who are all very opinionated.

I thought my time was very limited because of my heart disease, so I started taking measures to prepare for the worst. It seemed bad enough that I figured I should sell the farm as quickly as I could. You need a good income to sustain that sort of living, and I didn't want to leave my wife and kids with a big ownership they couldn't afford.

So we decided to move back to the city. It was intriguing. The oil man who had owned the farm before us had wanted to move to ours in the city because it was right next to the hospital. And here I was, years later, doing the exact same thing. And to my surprise, the house was available. When I got sick, my sister-in-law called to tell me that the oil man had died and that his widow was looking to sell the house, the same house we traded for initially, the one with the busy street caddy corner from George's house. It was too big for her now.

It was a great opportunity for me. George still lived in his house and so moving there would put me closer to him and closer to the hospital. I sold the farm, very quickly (and very cheaply), so that I could purchase the old house. We moved into it hoping we wouldn't have to redo anything, because I thought Darla had already done everything to it that it would ever need. I was mistaken; she had to redo a lot of other things.

We lived in that house for a good period of time, but Darla developed breast cancer. After a few years of living in the old house, Darla told me that she really wanted us to consider moving into another house, one with a first-floor bedroom. We thought about it for a while, but we didn't end up moving until a few more years after that.

In the meantime, in 1994, we went to Phoenix to see the kids (two of our daughters went to ASU and loved it so much they decided to stay), and Darla decided she wanted a house here. We started looking, but I wasn't as enthusiastic about buying another house as Darla was. We looked and looked but I kept saying "no" to each house we went to. But Darla was a very clever lady, and she knew me very well. She played to my strengths and my weaknesses and ultimately she convinced me to make an offer on a house in Arizona that we both kind of liked. She was very smart in that she never tried to overrule my decisions, instead always making me feel that I was making the final decision. The offer I made was ridiculously low and I thought for sure that they'd refuse it. But after I made the offer, they said yes, and I was on the hook to buy it. So we bought it and Darla redid that one, too. She spent the whole summer around 1994 in Arizona redoing that house. I wasn't there; I went back to Wichita for the summer. She re-landscaped it, increased the patio, painted the house, and fixed a few things, all by herself. We still own it, and nothing has changed since then, except a year ago, when my daughter decided to redo the guest house with my permission.

The next year, 1996, we tried looking around our neighborhood in Wichita, called "College Hill," for a house that would better suit Darla's changing medical needs. College Hill was full of huge, gorgeous homes that we loved, but I don't think any of them had first-floor bedrooms. I don't understand what the builders were thinking with that. So we started looking for houses elsewhere. We found the right one a little while later. It was a shell—it wasn't finished—but it was big and it had the potential to be beautiful. It was basically Darla's dream. She bought it and she finished it, doing a lot of things in the house including the kitchen. And, as always, she did a truly magnificent job with it.

After I lost Darla to her breast cancer on May 30, 2003, I was extremely lonely, the loneliest I've ever felt in my life. Even though I expected it would happen, I really wasn't ready for it. You can know that someone is dying and have no idea what it's going to be like once they are gone. She really was the best wife I could have ever hoped for and she was the best mother for our children. But you didn't even have to be in the family to fall in love with her. She really lit up the room wherever she went. She is missed a great deal by a great many people.

It was bittersweet to me that Darla only suffered for the

final three or four months of her life. It was very difficult to let her go, but it was also difficult to see her in pain. The first few months after her death were the worst for me. I sunk into a low depression, and I had a hard time pulling myself out of it at first. But then I reminded myself that I only had a short time left myself, and that I needed to make the most of it while I still could. Darla would have wanted that, anyway. And so I've led an active social life since my wife's death. I began to go out, see people. I reengaged with the people in my life, and got to know new ones, in a short period of time. I think I made the right decision, choosing to be happy rather than to grieve over conditions beyond my control.

After Darla passed, I also realized that I was not actually on the verge of death like I had thought so many years before. I had even outlived my wife. I went to the Cleveland Clinic to see what the situation was. I expected my coronaries to be terrible, just as they were nine years before. But they did another heart cath, and they told me my longevity was going to be normal. I had beat the odds. I lost a lot of weight because I began living appropriately—eating right and exercising—and it had paid off.

The doctors warned me that I would be a little restricted in what I could or couldn't do. If I wanted to do more, they were willing to operate and I would have that freedom. But if I was happy with what I was doing, there was no reason to operate because I was still going to have a normal longevity. I didn't want surgery. I knew it very well and I knew its potentials and its dangers, so I opted to stick with my lifestyle the way that it was.

Now that I knew I had more time on my hands, I decided to get more involved with the community. After retiring, I had tried my hand at being an internist and doing consultations, but that didn't work out. So instead, I got interested in the YMCA and I've done a fair amount of things with them. I helped them to create sport centers for children to play basketball and volleyball and other various activities in. Twenty-five years ago the YMCA was about to go broke, but then a gentleman, Dennis

Schoenebeck, took over. We went from serving 20,000 people a year to serving 20,000 people a day. The YMCA in Kansas is now the number one YMCA in the nation, and maybe even the world. Close to half of the county belongs in the YMCA. There are seven or eight YMCA centers in the county and each of them is huge. Some exceed 115,000 square feet. There are three sport centers, some of which are 112,000 square feet. It really has come a long way, and I hope that I've been a small factor in that.

I do a lot of other things with my time, too. I manage some of the kids' money. I manage George's affairs and his estate; he died in January 2014. I've also done a lot of the normal retiree activities. I traveled to Las Vegas. I enjoy working out. I have taken up golf the last twenty years. Last year I played more golf than I played in my whole life. Needless to say I'm a very poor golfer.

I feel fortunate with my life especially now that I'm older. I've learned to appreciate the little things. I thank God for each time I wake up. Each day is great – I'm awake and walking to the breakfast table. So many of my colleagues and friends can't even do that anymore. Family is so very important. George and his wife Brenda have four lovely daughters and several grandchildren. I want to express my heart-felt gratitude to Brenda for her love and devotion to my brother and for the care she gave him at the end of his life.

I have four wonderful children, Maria, Mark, Todd and Tiffany, who are very successful in their chosen fields. I am very proud of each of my children and all they have accomplished. I am also very proud of my sons-in-law Ken and Brock and daughters-in-law Erin and Dina. I am fortunate to have six beautiful granddaughters, Carly, Kelsey, Maya, Avery, Emerson and Lilia. I think you have to be a grandparent to truly understand the happiness that comes with having grandchildren and the joy I have in hearing them call me "Jiddi" (which is Arabic for Grandfather).

Every Christmas Eve my brother George would make a toast "It's a great life!" My life isn't perfect, but it's about as near as you can get.

* * *

I consider myself one of the luckiest people because I am an American citizen. I do not see people wanting to leave America but many millions want to come here. The greatest thing I have gained is having personal freedom – Liberty. Liberty is the fuel of success. I have learned three important things that I think about often.

The first is that we live in the greatest country on the face of the earth. The second thing is marriage can succeed in spite of significant differences, if a couple is willing to discuss all issues on the table and be willing to listen.

And the last thing is immigrants that come to the USA to achieve and better themselves can achieve the American Dream, which in my opinion is alive and well for those that have "fire in their belly".

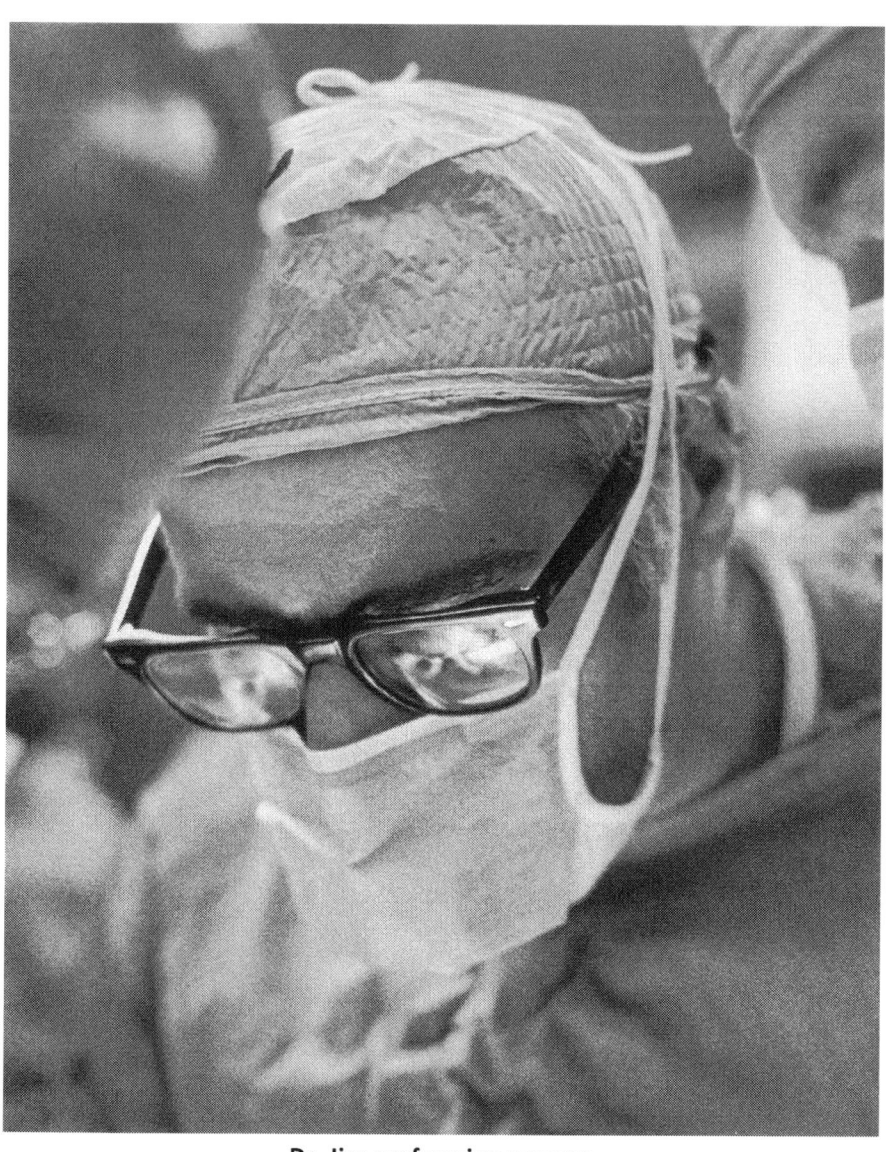

Dr. Jim performing surgery

Dr. George

Wadia Mikhael Farha and Jamil Farhat Farha (parents)

Dr. Jim and Dr. George at retirement from Wichita Surgical Specialists

Farha family portrait.
Back row: (L to R) Doug Malone, Ken and Maria Blewster, David and Joan Farha, Dr. George Farha, Dr. Jim Farha, Mark Farha, Todd Farha, Laura Farha, Brock Oaks; Front row: (L to R) Gayle Malone, Julie Farha, Brenda Farha, Darla Farha, Tiffany Farha

(L to R) Dr. George and Brenda Farha, Dr. Jim and Darla Farha

Darla and Dr. Jim

Darla Farha, Violette Ammar and Brenda Farha

(L to R) Majed Farha, Violette Ammar, Ghassan Farha, Dr. George Farha, Ghaleb Farha, Dr. Jim Farha with great nephew and niece

Back row: Darla and Dr. Jim Farha; Front row (L to R) Dr. George Farha,
Violette Ammar and Wadia Farha (mother)

Dr. Jim and Darla with children – Darla's 59th birthday party.
Back row: Mark, Dr. Jim, Ken and Maria
Front row: Tiffany, Brock, Darla, Todd

Bill Shdeed, Dr. George Farha and Dr. Jim Farha

Dr. Jim with Violette Ammar (sister)

(L to R) Jamil Malone, Doug Malone, Dr. Jim and Michael Malone

Greater Wichita YMCA ribbon cutting ceremony for one of the Farha Sport Centers. Todd Farha (second from left) Dr. Jim (cutting ribbon)

Dr. Jim and Bubba

Dr. Jim at dedication of one of the Farha Sport Centers at Greater Wichita YMCA

Dr. Jim with twin granddaughters Avery and Emerson Oaks

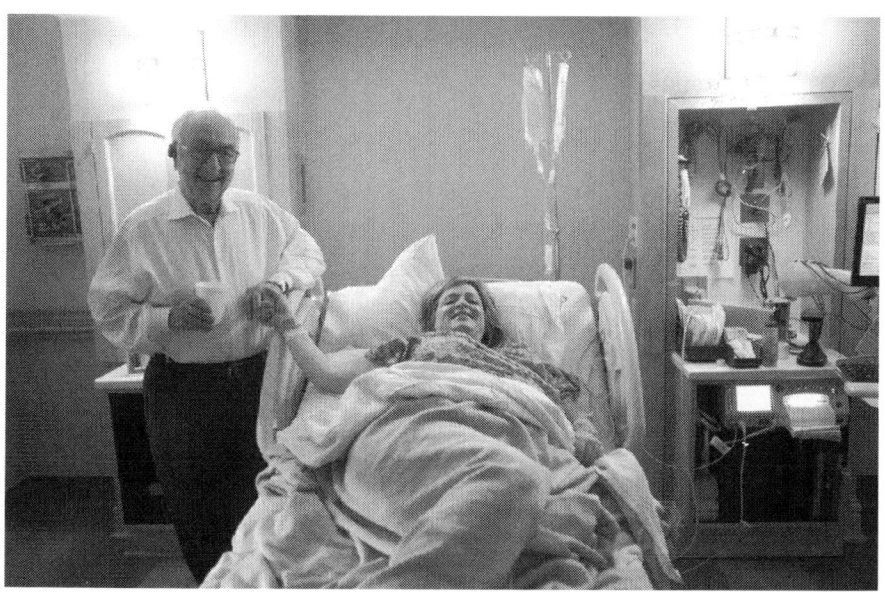

Dr. Jim and daughter Tiffany Farha

Christmas Party at Dr. Jim's home. Back row: Brock and Emerson Oaks, Dina, Mark and Maya Farha, Erin Stuart and Todd Farha, Maria Farha Blewster; Front row: Tiffany Farha and Avery Oaks, Muna and Asaad Rahhal, S. Jamil Farha (Dr. Jim), Carly Blewster, Ken Blewster and Kelsey Blewster.

Family portrait at Second Street home.
Back row: Maria Farha, Todd Farha and Mark Farha;
Front row: Dr. Jim and Darla Farha, and Tiffany Farha

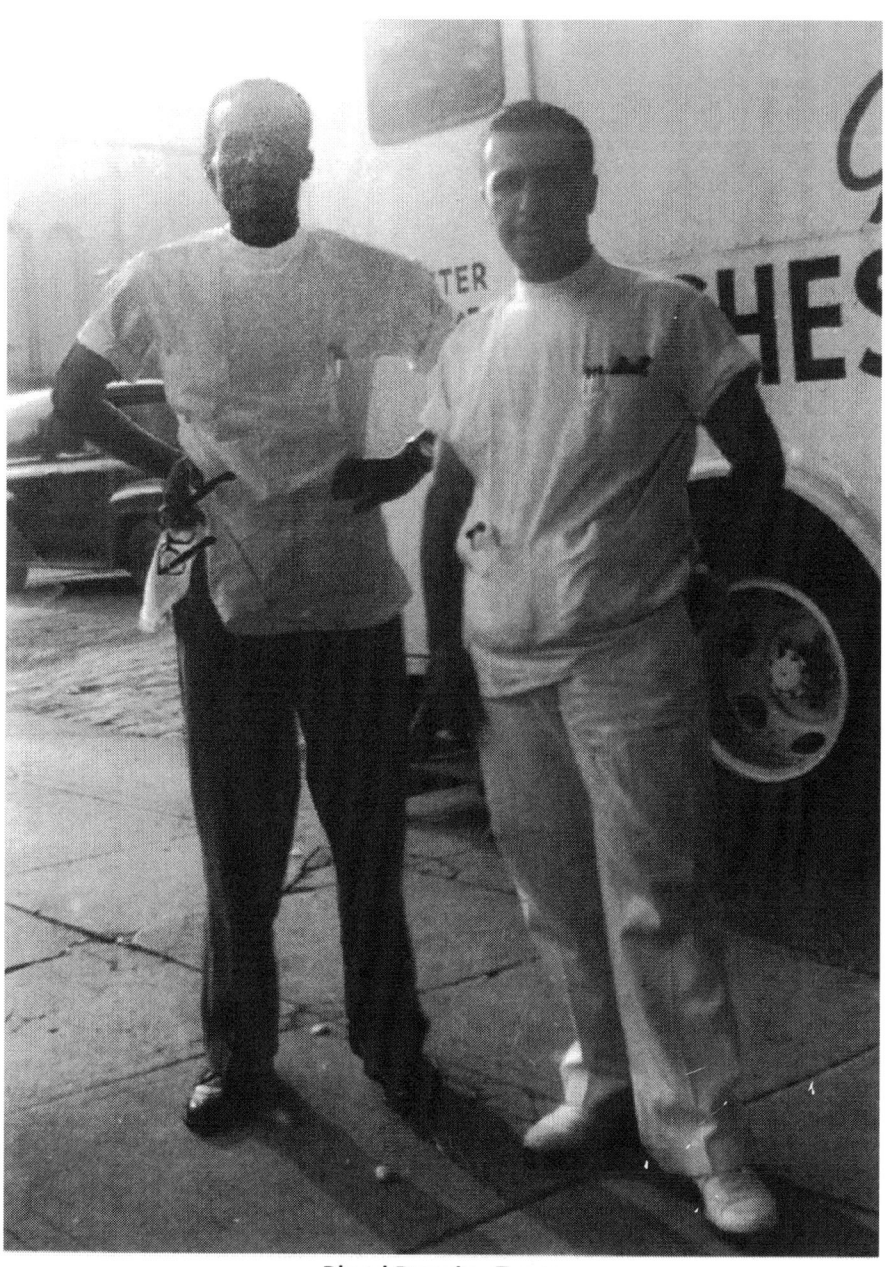

Blood Drawing Team
"Medical Students Hungry for Blood" by the Washington Post, around 1955
Dr. George Farha and Dr. S. Jim Farha

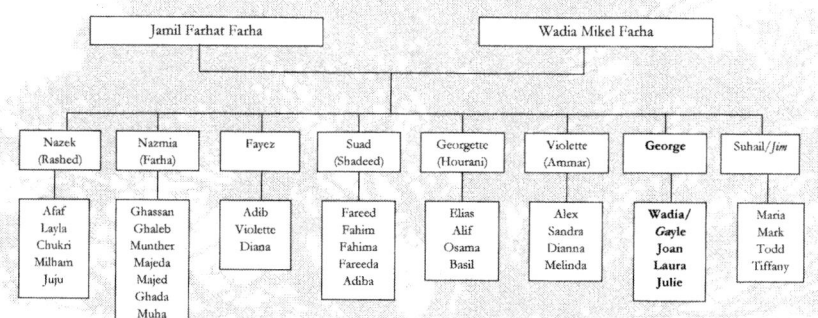

George Jamil Farha

Jamil Farhat Farha	Wadia Mikel Farha

Nazek (Rashed)	Nazmia (Farha)	Fayez	Suad (Shadeed)	Georgette (Hourani)	Violette (Ammar)	**George**	Suhail/*Jim*
Afaf Layla Chukri Milham Juju	Ghassan Ghaleb Munther Majeda Majed Ghada Muha	Adib Violette Diana	Fareed Fahim Fahima Fareeda Adiba	Elias Alif Osama Basil	Alex Sandra Dianna Melinda	**Wadia/** *Gayle* **Joan** **Laura** **Julie**	Maria Mark Todd Tiffany

The Origins of the Farha Family and its Name

The Farha family has its origins with the earliest Christians called the "Ghassasnids" or in Arabic al-Ghassasnah, also Banu Ghassan," Tribe of Ghassan," which was in fact a Kingdom from 220 A.D. until 712 A.D. They were located in Yemen until between the Third and Fourth Century A.D. when they started to migrate to the Levant (Lebanon and Syria). Some say they originally came from the Levant where they were Christianized by St. Paul afterwards going to Yemen, but for sure they finally settled in Lebanon and Syria.

The Kingdom of Ghassan became part of the Byzantine Empire and when Islam came in the Seventh Century, the Ghassasnids maintained their Christian faith. Christians of the Middle East were of the Eastern rite and when Rome and Constantinople split in 1054, they were either Greek Orthodox or Greek Melkite Catholic, the latter eventually coming under the jurisdiction of the Pope in Rome. Most of the Farha family today are either Greek Orthodox or Greek Catholic, but in any event have remained Christian.

The last Ghassasnid King was called Ghassan Al Hourani whose rule ended in 712 A.D. His family name Is particularly interesting since it indicates he was born from Houran, a province in Syria near Lebanon, which is where the Farha family name originated.

The name "Farha" was actually the first name of a woman. Her husband's family name is not altogether certain, but it was believed to be Rashid. In any event, he died leaving his wife Farha with a number of children, including the three sons shown on the Family Tree, Issa (Jesus in Arabic), Ibrahim (Abraham) and Hanna (John).

My father's branch stems from Issa and my mother's (also a

Farha) from Ibrahim. Actually, there are many family names today from the Lavant which are the first names of women, such as Ablah, Samara, Jabara, and Hamra, all ending in the letter "a," indicating the female gender in Arabic. Apparently, it was common for the men to marry much younger women and when they died, a strong-minded widow could have her first name as the family name.

In the year 1635, when the Farha family lived in Izra, a town in Houran, Syria, the Ottomans were carrying out a purge against Christians. So the Farha's fled to Lebanon on the other side of Mount Hermon to the province of Marjayoun, which was a Christian area and in the Roman Empire known as Caesarea Philippi.

Marjayoun has two cathedrals in its capital of Jedeidet, the Greek Melkite Catholic St. Peter and the Greek Orthodox St. George each having its own archbishop. Always an important Christian area, there were also Shi'a and Sunni Muslims in Marjayoun and when the Farha family arrived there in 1635 the famous ruler of Lebanon at the time, Sheikh Fakr Al-Din, who was a Druze, made no distinction between religions, all having equal rights and freedom to live without persecution.

In 2007, when visiting Syria, I went to Izra, in Houran and in the Greek Catholic church named St. Elias, built in the Sixth Century A.D. under the Emperor Justinian, the priest from that church knew about the Farha family and other Christians who fled Izra for Marjayoun and even confirmed the date being 1635.

Alfred S. Farha   Thalwil/Zürich, Switzerland   April 15th 2015

Printed in Great Britain
by Amazon